Items should be returned on or before the last date shown below. Items not already requested by other borrowers may be renewed in person, in writing or by telephone. To renew, please quote the number on the barcode label. To renew online a PIN is required. This can be requested at your local library.
Renew online @ **www.dublincitypubliclibraries.ie**
Fines charged for overdue items will include postage incurred in recovery. Damage to or loss of items will be charged to the borrower.

Leabharlanna Poiblí Chathair Bhaile Átha Cliath
Dublin City Public Libraries

Baile Átha Cliath
Dublin City

Date Due	Date Due	Date Due
0 3 JUL 2018		

D0785988

❖ **Also in the Hay House Basics series** ❖

Crystals

Mindfulness

Past Lives

Angels

Lucid Dreaming

Tarot

Energy Healing

NLP

Self-Hypnosis

Coming soon

Numerology

Feng Shui

Shamanism

Astrology

REIKI

Heal Your Body and Your Life with the Power of Universal Energy

TORSTEN A. LANGE

HAY HOUSE

Carlsbad, California • New York City • London • Sydney
Johannesburg • Vancouver • Hong Kong • New Delhi

First published and distributed in the United Kingdom by:
Hay House UK Ltd, Astley House, 33 Notting Hill Gate, London W11 3JQ
Tel: +44 (0)20 3675 2450; Fax: +44 (0)20 3675 2451; www.hayhouse.co.uk

Published and distributed in the United States of America by:
Hay House Inc., PO Box 5100, Carlsbad, CA 92018-5100
Tel: (1) 760 431 7695 or (800) 654 5126; Fax: (1) 760 431 6948 or (800) 650 5115
www.hayhouse.com

Published and distributed in Australia by:
Hay House Australia Ltd, 18/36 Ralph St, Alexandria NSW 2015
Tel: (61) 2 9669 4299; Fax: (61) 2 9669 4144; www.hayhouse.com.au

Published and distributed in the Republic of South Africa by:
Hay House SA (Pty) Ltd, PO Box 990, Witkoppen 2068
info@hayhouse.co.za

Published and distributed in India by:
Hay House Publishers India, Muskaan Complex, Plot No.3, B-2,
Vasant Kunj, New Delhi 110 070
Tel: (91) 11 4176 1620; Fax: (91) 11 4176 1630; www.hayhouse.co.in

Distributed in Canada by:
Raincoast Books, 2440 Viking Way, Richmond, B.C. V6V 1N2
Tel: (1) 604 448 7100; Fax: (1) 604 270 7161; www.raincoast.com

Text © Torsten A. Lange, 2015

A catalogue record for this book is available from the British Library.

Some names in this book have been changed to
protect the privacy of individuals.

ISBN: 978-1-78180-555-8

Interior illustrations: 26, 27, 34, 76–77, 93–95, 119, 128, 168, 169
Alexa Garside/www.brightonillustrators.co.uk; 37, 159, 162, 165, 181,
229 Torsten A. Lange; All other images canstockphoto.com

Printed and bound in Great Britain by TJ International, Padstow, Cornwall.

For Dad,
who almost died the day before
I started to write this book.
The doctors called his recovery a miracle.
But the miracle had a name: Reiki.

Contents

List of exercises

Preface

Ten years ago I didn't believe in Reiki. In fact, I didn't believe in anything that I would classify as esoteric, spiritual or even alternative. I preferred to keep my feet firmly on the ground. That is, until the ground suddenly disappeared.

After a career as a successful entrepreneur, with businesses in Germany and the UK, a flagship store on London's Regent Street and an export venture to the USA, I found my life falling apart almost overnight. I was made bankrupt and homeless, and after years of struggle was on the brink of ending my life.

Reiki pieced it back together. In fact, my circumstances started to improve the very day it came into my life. Luckily, it doesn't matter whether you believe in Reiki or not: it still works. I found a new job, was given the opportunity to become a Reiki Master and eventually founded the Reiki Academy London. It is certainly no exaggeration to say that Reiki has been the most amazing discovery of my life.

But when our life crashes, it tends to affect others as well. Dad was among those who felt it most. After all, it wasn't just my own home that was lost, but the family home in

Hamburg as well. And yet he was the way he'd always been towards me: loving and supportive. How I wished I could give him something in return!

With Reiki putting my life slowly back on track, this became more feasible. Dad and his wife came on holiday to the UK and we spent some lovely days together by the sea.

I had so many plans for the future – and then a phone call came out of the blue: Dad had gone into hospital for minor surgery and it had revealed a rare infection: necrotizing fasciitis. He might not survive the night.

All I could do was give him Reiki. Of course I was nowhere near him, but little problems like that don't matter with Reiki – it can be sent over any distance, no matter how far.

When using Reiki, we tend to feel a physical sensation in our hands, but I'd only felt this particular way once before: when I'd sent Reiki to a cancer patient in the final stages of the disease. He had died the following day. There was no doubt that Dad was in a life-or-death struggle too. When I went to bed, I asked for Reiki to carry on being sent through the night and fell asleep feeling my hands beaming healing energy across the continent.

Dad had a second operation the following evening, a Friday. Throughout the day, my entire family was sending Reiki, fuelled by the distressing information a Google search had provided on the illness: chances of survival were slim, treatment difficult, lasting impairment almost guaranteed.

Over the weekend, though, Dad's condition started to improve, and by the time I finally arrived at his bedside on Sunday, it was clear that he would survive. He wouldn't even lose his leg, as some of the doctors had expected. My sister arrived, we gave him Reiki treatments together, and what we saw was a miracle happening before our very eyes: his complexion was becoming fresher by the hour and he was eating and talking and even joking. The next day, he walked a few steps on crutches. Five doctors were watching in awe. None of them had anticipated such a speedy recovery. Or possibly any recovery.

Two more operations followed to remove the affected tissue and two weeks later Dad left hospital. Today there is nothing left but a very long scar and we can still hardly believe our luck. We are just as amazed as the doctors. But this is what miracles do: the impossible.

Having trained hundreds of students now at the Reiki Academy London, I witness Reiki bringing miracles on an almost daily basis. Few things are more exciting for me than watching the expression of disbelief in the students' eyes when they use their 'healing hands' for the first time. It works!

And yet even miracles don't always turn out to be exactly what we hoped for. I'm certain that Dad's recovery was the result of receiving Reiki. But this doesn't lead to the automatic conclusion that Reiki works like that all the time.

What would I have done if Dad had died? Would I still have finished this book? I'm glad this question is rhetorical! But it needs to be answered nevertheless. Yes, I would have finished this book. Because healing doesn't always mean curing. An illness may even be good for us, helping us to learn and change. And, after all, death isn't the end.

Reiki has much to say about this. In fact, it's only through questions like this that it can be properly understood. It is a complementary therapy, but it goes beyond that. Far, far beyond.

This story, of course, is rather personal – and pretty intense. But it feels right to share it, because Reiki is always personal. And always intense. If you're already practising Reiki or have had a Reiki treatment, I'm certain you'll agree. If you're about to learn Reiki, I can pretty much guarantee that you'll soon be having the most incredible experiences. Because Reiki is neither an esoteric discourse nor an antiseptic theory. It's personal, practical and experiential. Warm, loving and life-changing. And incredibly deep.

Introduction

So what actually is Reiki?

More than you think

Reiki is one of the most popular energy-healing systems in the world. Founded in Japan in the early 20th century, it is simple to learn and everyone who has been attuned to it can use it. It's truly mind-boggling: you book on a Reiki course and hours later walk home with 'healing hands', the trademark feature of Reiki.

Reiki is easy to learn – but also easily misunderstood. Beyond the simplicity of its methods lies enormous depth. If we want to understand it properly, we need to look at it as both an alternative therapy *and* a spiritual path. Even if we concentrate on one, the other is always present. What makes Reiki so unique is that the two are closely interwoven: healing and personal development cannot be separated.

And indeed, this is how it all started: with the spiritual development of one person, a Japanese man called Mikao Usui, who, to his own surprise, eventually found himself with healing hands. But, rather than styling himself as a super healer, he thought: *If I can do it, others should be able to as well. After all, the entire world needs healing!* So he created a system that could be learned by absolutely everyone. One could say that he democratized palm healing. It isn't exclusive to saints and shamans any more – it's open to you and me. (And if you *are* a saint, you'll still benefit from it.)

And yet when it comes to explaining exactly what Reiki is and how it works, most people are at a loss. Practitioners normally feel a physical sensation in their hands and recipients often experience strong sensations of warmth or energy movement, but there can be a confusing variety of results.

For Dad, Reiki brought physical healing. But it didn't stop there. His thoughts soon moved from *I've survived!* to *Why have I survived? What am I supposed to learn from this? What am I supposed to change?* While waiting for the car to take him home from hospital, he phoned me and said, 'I definitely won't carry on living as I have before. There's so much I've started to understand now...'

Sometimes, though, the effects are very simple. My student Anthony, for instance, had a son with sleeping problems. For the whole nine years of his life the boy had been waking Anthony and his wife at least once every night: 'Mum, Dad, I can't sleep!' After his first Reiki course, Anthony started to give him Reiki just before bedtime. He now sleeps through the night!

Indeed, Reiki is often described as a method for relaxation and stress reduction. But there is more to it than that.

Patty, a primary school teacher, was in charge of the school playground when a little girl fell and cut her chin. Taking her to the first-aid room, she decided to place her hand near her face and give her Reiki. When they met the first-aider, they were greeted with puzzlement. Why all the fuss? And indeed, the bleeding had stopped and the cut had already half healed. I just love hearing stories like this at my monthly Reiki Shares (*see page 117*).

Unsurprisingly, Reiki is now used in many hospitals and even recommended to reduce the side effects of cancer treatments. But there is still more.

A lady joined one of my courses after she'd had a beauty treatment. Apparently she'd looked so tired and sad that the beautician had decided creams and make-up wouldn't be enough. As a trained Reiki practitioner, she'd asked whether she could add a few minutes of Reiki to the end of the session. Her client was gobsmacked by what followed: closing her eyes, she saw different colours, felt warm and relaxed – and found a wave of love washing over her. A few weeks later she joined the Reiki course and started to deal with a recent bereavement and decades of trauma. I'd never seen such a stark change in facial expression over the course of a single weekend before. She arrived looking as though she'd given up on life and left radiating relaxation and happiness and with an almost constant smile. A few weeks later, she mentioned that her husband simply couldn't believe how much she'd changed.

And yet we can go still further. If you're already used to Reiki, you may not even be surprised by the story a lady told me about her first Reiki treatment. Lying on the treatment couch, she suddenly felt the presence of her mother, who had passed away a few years before. They had a long conversation and the mother gave a detailed message for the lady's brother: he should be careful at a place called Golden Oak. The lady duly passed this information on, but her brother, a policeman, only knew of a pub of that name, and it wasn't one he'd go in anyway. However, a few weeks later he was called to a house in Golden Oak Avenue, where a schizophrenic man was causing trouble. As he approached the man, he remembered the warning and slowed down – at which point the man suddenly produced a knife and tried to stab him. Without the warning, he would have been severely injured at least.

For another lady, the most exciting experience after her first Reiki course was comparatively simple: an encounter with a bumblebee. Lying on its back, it appeared more dead than alive. Gently turning it over, my student placed her hand over it and gave it a few minutes of Reiki, after which it happily flew off.

Reiki works in a myriad ways. No wonder it can be confusing! Why does one person find it helps to reconcile them with their partner and another person find it gives them the strength to divorce? Why do the results differ from person to person? Why does it work for so many different problems? And, question of questions, how does it *technically* work?

I've met quite a few people who've found this so challenging that they've actually walked away from it. And frankly, I almost did this myself. My intellect was asking, 'How can I use something I cannot explain?' But my heart was saying,

'It simply feels right.' And I couldn't deny the physical sensation – and the results.

This is what Reiki is famous for. It's not about theory, it's about tangible results. It's not about belief, it's about proof.

And I would like to add that we *can* reconcile our heart and our intellect.

Getting the facts right

If we want to understand a tradition, the natural starting-point is its historical beginnings. With Reiki, though, this used to be a tricky endeavour. For over half a century its history was shrouded in mystery. As it was taught as an oral tradition, little of it was historically verifiable. Over time, the accounts changed and expanded and Reiki itself was combined with other techniques and philosophies. The result was like a game of Chinese whispers (or rather, Japanese), and the history of Reiki became almost fiction. But now we finally have new information about its origins.

It turned out that much information had been kept secret by a small group of Japanese Reiki Teachers. Only since the 1990s has this gradually come out into the open. Today we have three main sources for this additional information:

1. The *Usui memorial stone*, erected in 1927, a year after the death of Mikao Usui. Located in the grounds of the Saihoji Temple in Tokyo, it became known to Westerners only in the 1990s. It gives a host of information about Usui's life and has provided a starting-point for historical research.

2. The *Usui Reiki Ryoho Gakkai*, the original Reiki training organization. Founded in the 1920s, this has provided (albeit somewhat involuntarily) amazing information.

3. Accounts from *contemporaries and students* of Mikao Usui. These have now been unearthed and *other Japanese Reiki traditions* (in addition to the Gakkai) have come to light.

Based on this information, Chapter 1 of this book, 'The history of Reiki', relates the remarkable life story of Mikao Usui, which offers plenty of opportunities to reflect on similarities in our own lives. It also examines the cultural and spiritual influences on the Reiki system and the key discovery: that the system of Reiki is the result of a moment of enlightenment.

The next step would normally be to look at the system itself. But since it was designed in the 1920s, science has taken a big leap forward and, quite rightly, today Reiki is subject to close scrutiny. So, is there a scientific basis for it? Is there an explanation of how it works? This is what we'll explore in the next two chapters, 'Energy' and 'Healing'.

We'll see that 'energy' really describes *everything* – and shows how everything is *interconnected*. This provides a basis for understanding how Reiki works. We'll also look at what it means for us, for *we* are energy too. Energy is of importance not only for the body but also for the entire universe. After all, *rei* and *ki* mean 'universal energy'.

The second keyword is 'healing'. Of course this is what we look for when we use a healing system. But what does it actually *mean*? This chapter introduces the different levels of healing, offers a holistic understanding and ultimately touches on how Reiki can help us find meaning in our existence and so heal not only our body but our whole life.

Getting practical

I call the above 'the basics'. Exploring them can help enormously in making sense of Reiki. But, as I never tire of repeating, Reiki is about *experience*. And this comes when we actually *use* the techniques.

So this book provides a comprehensive overview of the system Mikao Usui created, based on the latest research. I am going back to the roots with the aim to free Reiki from the add-ons, the myths and the fiction that have changed the system over the years. As so often, I tend to find the original still works best.

First, in Chapter 4, we have a quick look at the structure of the system: the three levels of training. We also examine the elements around which the system is designed: attunements; palm healing; symbols and mantras; breathing, cleansing and meditation; the five Reiki principles and Waka poetry.

Although the elements are consistent throughout the levels of training, I have singled out the attunements and consider them first, in Chapter 5, before we look at the different levels in depth. After all, the attunements (or initiations) are the mind-blowing speciality of Reiki. A short ritual is all it takes for students to establish a personal connection to Reiki. Once they've been attuned in this way, they can feel a physical sensation in their palms, become aware of an inner spiritual connection and use Reiki to heal themselves and others. The closer we get to an understanding of the attunements, the closer we get to understanding Reiki.

Reiki 1 (*Shoden* in Japanese), the first level of Reiki, which is explored in Chapters 6, 7 and 8, covers the basics of using the system. In Chapter 6, the technical aspects are shown in step-by-step exercises, including how to give a complete Reiki treatment. This covers the foundations of Reiki treatment on all levels. We also look at the common effects on clients – we don't want the practitioner left as puzzled as the recipient afterwards! (Although it has to be said that Reiki often brings something new, even for the most seasoned practitioner.)

Chapter 7 looks at meditation, breathing and energy cleansing and includes many original techniques that were only recently rediscovered. They can deepen the experience of Reiki in absolutely amazing ways.

Chapter 8 completes our look at the first level of Reiki with an explanation of the Reiki principles and the use of poetry and spiritual texts in the system – simple tools to bring Reiki into everyday life.

Reiki 2 (*Okuden*), the next level, which is covered in Chapter 9, introduces the famous Reiki symbols – not just their use, but also the amazing concept behind them. I also include advanced palm-healing techniques and take a brief look at practising Reiki professionally.

Finally, in Chapter 10, we look at the Master level (*Shinpiden*) and discover that Reiki is a path to *enlightenment*. This chapter sums up the ultimate goal of Reiki and brings all the previous techniques and stages together.

And more...

The last section of the book is dedicated to notes for and from Reiki practice. It covers frequently asked questions and anything else I haven't managed to squeeze into the previous chapters.

I have also included an appendix on the development of Reiki after the death of Mikao Usui. A Further Reading section and index are also provided at the end of the book.

I would like to mention that most of the time I use the terms 'Reiki', 'system of Reiki' and 'Usui system of Reiki' interchangeably. They all refer to the system created by Mikao Usui. I have made it clear when I use the word 'Reiki' to refer to the energy rather than the system.

And finally, I would like to stress that this book does not replace a Reiki course. Reiki always needs to be kick-started with an attunement – a one-to-one energy transfer. This is what makes it so special. Luckily, Reiki teachers can be found all over the globe. I'm sure you'll find the right one for you.

Part I
THE BASICS

'There are only two mistakes one can make along the road to truth: not going all the way, and not starting.'

BUDDHA

Chapter 1
The history of Reiki

As with many great spiritual traditions, Reiki started with just one person: Mikao Usui. Born on 15 August 1865, he was smart, eloquent and well read. But, as we all know from personal experience, this isn't everything. We also need a dose of luck – and when this goes missing, we can reach rock bottom. Mikao Usui did. But if he hadn't, we wouldn't have the gift of Reiki.

Mikao Usui, the founder

His early life

Quite a few people who practise Reiki divide their lives into *before* and *after* Reiki. I will apply the same to Mikao Usui – after all, his life *before* Reiki provided the ground in which it could blossom. As this isn't a history book, I'll try to keep this account short. But here are what I consider the six key points about this time:

1. A time of change

Usui was born into a time of tremendous cultural and political change. After centuries of almost complete isolation, the country was being opened to trade and international contacts by the new Japanese emperor, who even invited other cultures to send envoys and teachers, including Christian missionaries. Internally, the changes were just as drastic: democracy was introduced, and education, health, industrial production and science exploded. The period is commonly called the Meiju Restoration, named after the emperor. It catapulted Japan to prosperity and international influence. The country said hello to the world.

2. Usui was a Samurai

Mikao Usui came from a Samurai family, the traditional ruling class. Prior to the Meiju period, the Samurai had been the only Japanese allowed to carry a surname – and the name 'Usui' has a particular history. In the 12th century, a famous Samurai warrior, Chiba Tsunetane, conquered the town of Usui and subsequently all the members of his clan had this as their surname.

This tradition seems to be of such significance that Mikao Usui's ancestry is mentioned on his memorial stone. But he was born at the wrong time: the Meiju Restoration scrapped all the traditional privileges and brought in a system of equal opportunity for all. The Samurai's exclusive access to jobs in government, administration and the police was abolished and they now had to make as much effort to establish themselves in a career as everyone else. Still, it is certainly fair to assume that Usui was brought up in the

Samurai tradition of endurance, philosophical reflection and the practice of martial arts.

3. Rice wine drying up
In any case, there was no need for him to be worried about the loss of privileges – his own future was settled. His family was comparatively well off and as the eldest son of four children (he had one sister and two brothers), he was set to inherit the *sake* brewery owned by his grandfather. His family also owned a trading business.

However, during Usui's time much changed and even this security did not last for long. His grandfather had signed an affidavit for a friend that could not be paid back. He lost the brewery.

4. Two kinds of Buddhism
There doesn't seem to have been much else in the little village of Taniai, where the Usuis lived. Located in the Gifu district, a mountainous region in southern Japan, it didn't even have a school.

As a young boy, therefore, Mikao Usui would have been educated by the monks at the nearby monastery. This was common practice in the absence of a school. The monastery belonged to Pure Land Buddhism, one of the big Buddhist teaching traditions in Japan, but the monks would have also taught general knowledge.

In his teens, Usui would have continued his education at a school in a larger town. As the dominant denomination in the region was Zen Buddhism (his local monastery being only a little Pure Land enclave), this would have meant that during his youth he would have been made aware that it was possible (indeed the norm) to have the same creed yet different paths.

While Pure Land Buddhism is centred around the devotion to the Amida Buddha and the help of bodhisattvas (enlightened beings in the spirit world who act as helpers for humans), Zen focuses on meditation, experiential exploration and one-to-one teaching from a master. Both traditions later contributed elements to Usui's system of Reiki.

5. Big city, big politics
Finishing school, Usui was left without a clear career path as the brewery was gone. So he and one of his younger brothers moved to Tokyo, trying their luck in the big city. His brother became a medical doctor; Mikao Usui didn't. In fact, we don't really know what he became, or if he even had any formal education in Tokyo.

He was smart and ambitious, though, and keen on expanding his knowledge. Eventually he found a position that fitted his interests and personality: as the personal assistant of Shinpei Goto, who to this day is one of the most revered politicians in Japanese history. A trained medical doctor, he became an official in the health department and drew up new guidelines for public health, then went on to become health minister, minister for transport and information, interior secretary and foreign secretary. He was also the first civilian governor of Taiwan, headed the Manchurian Railway and eventually became mayor of Tokyo. He shared his Samurai background with Usui as well as a keen interest in the personal development of the individual – he was, for example, the first head of the Boy Scout movement in Japan. When, as mayor of Tokyo, he was presented with the prototype of an affordable watch, he declared that one day every citizen should be able to own one – and called the watch itself 'citizen'. Following the astonishing success of the product, this was later adopted as the company name.

It is not hard to imagine the influence such a man would have had on Mikao Usui, who was eight years younger. Goto would have clearly demonstrated that a combination of determination and values creates the basis for success.

There was another benefit to Usui's position too: he could travel. The memorial stone mentions that he visited the USA, Europe and China. So he would have been able to study different cultures and religions, and may have realized that no matter where they were in the world, people were faced with the same challenges. On the one hand, they were struggling with survival and everyday life; on the other, looking for meaning and truth. They may have used different names and symbols, but they were all on the same path.

All this knowledge bore fruit later on, when Usui created the system of Reiki and made it accessible to all, regardless of religious or cultural differences.

6. His life implodes
We don't know how long Usui worked for Goto, but eventually he went his own way. He married a woman called Sadako Suzuki, had two children (son Fuji in 1908

and daughter Toshiko in 1913) and became an entrepreneur. There is no information on the type of business he started – in fact there are some suggestions that he tried several different careers – but it doesn't matter. It wasn't the kind of venture that was important for his development, but its result. And that was: complete failure.

Mikao Usui was made bankrupt. I can claim to be a bit of an expert on this subject, and it can easily be summed up as a nightmare. My knowledge, however, is limited to what it feels like in 21st-century London. We can only imagine what it would have meant 100 years earlier (approximately between 1915 and 1918), in a society based on social standing, reputation and achievement – and to a descendant of the proud Samurai...

Usui tried anything and everything to get back on his feet – after all, he had a family to provide for – but nothing worked out. The memorial states: 'He fell into great difficulties.'[1] Unsurprisingly, he became depressed and frustrated.

Embracing change

He started to reflect on his life. Was he maybe not meant to return to his old career? Did the universe have different plans for him? After all, he'd always been aware that there was more to life than just a mundane career. For many years he is said to have practised Shugendo, an esoteric discipline combining elements of Buddhism, Taoism and Shintoism. Some research suggests that he was already teaching a small group of students this practice. Was this the time to intensify his quest for spiritual development? Was it even an opportunity?

Although his decision doesn't seem to have been too warmly received by his family, he resolved to follow his inner calling. And joined a monastery.

I would like to pause here for a moment, as I feel that this is the perfect point to really connect with Mikao Usui. Difficult times tend to provide a turning-point in life and it was the same for Usui as it is for us today. Would I have found my way to Reiki without my bankruptcy? I doubt it. Would you, dear reader, have picked up this book if you hadn't needed healing – either for yourself or someone around you? Probably not. Times of change are times of development.

But even after a turning-point, life continues to have its ups and downs – and Mikao Usui was about to face another setback. He joined a Zen monastery, stayed there three long years – and ended up even more frustrated. He hadn't found what he was looking for. As far as he was concerned, it was another failure.

Finding Reiki

But what *was* he looking for? The answer to this can bring us a big step closer to understanding Reiki.

Mikao Usui wasn't looking for theory or intellectual understanding. He wanted to know with his *heart*. He wanted to *feel*. He knew there was a level of awareness beyond doubt and the need for rational explanation, a place where he could experience complete peace and harmony. Or simply just *be*. Today, this is often described as 'being in the now'. In Japanese Zen Buddhism, it is called *Anshin Ritsumei*.

But Usui hadn't been able to take the final step from *knowing about* something to *living and being* it. Discussing with his abbot what else he could do, he received the advice that the only way left was to *die*. Not intentionally – but at least to accept the possibility. We cannot take anything material with us when we die – and this is what Usui was asked to do: to leave everything behind, retreat to the mountains and follow a rigid discipline of meditation and deprivation. He would fast and, towards the end, possibly even abstain from drinking and sleeping. These are practices still followed by Eastern mountain ascetics today. The idea behind them is to give up anything that is normally considered essential in life and experience what lies beyond, eventually reaching a state of complete non-attachment or, in Buddhist terms, *Nirvana*. The saying goes that on that path you either find enlightenment or die.

Usui withdrew into complete isolation on Mount Kurama (*Kuramayama* in Japanese), a place well known by spiritual seekers. After three weeks the moment of transformation arrived: he felt as if he'd been struck by lightning. He had a vision of light so bright that he needed to close his eyes – and felt at complete peace with the world. He stopped identifying with his physical body, shed the boundaries of being individual and felt *one* with everything. *Reiki* is often translated as 'universal energy' – and at that moment Usui felt connected to the entire universe.

In Japanese this is called *satori*: a moment of sudden understanding, of looking beyond the illusionary veil of problems and seeing the world as it really is. In other words, a moment of enlightenment in a very literal sense: seeing the light. *Only* light. There is a complete absence of darkness, shadows, pain and desire. Pure being, pure bliss. Pure Nirvana. No theoretical understanding, no belief involved. Just experience. Just Reiki.

The mountain retreat had served its purpose. Usui was ready to go back. In fact, he probably couldn't wait to go back to share his experiences with his abbot and his family.

As he was leaving, a now-famous incident took place: he caught his foot on one of the many roots covering the mountain and tore off a toenail. (And it *did* hurt – after all, he was still attached to his body, still a human being.) When he leaned down to look at the wound, he placed his hands around the toe – and, to his surprise, it started to heal. He realized that enlightenment had brought him healing powers.

He carried on walking down the mountain and eventually stopped for refreshment at an inn at the bottom. When the innkeeper's daughter brought him a drink, he noticed that she was in great pain from a tooth infection. Realizing he might be able to heal this, or even just deciding to try things out, he asked for her father's permission to treat her, then placed his hands around her jaw – and both the pain and the swelling went down.

Mikao Usui had become a Reiki healer.

The system of Reiki

Now everything happened very quickly. Usui tried the palm healing on friends and family, moved his family back to Tokyo and within a month had opened a small healing practice there. But it wasn't his intention to be known as *the* miracle-healer. He didn't want to become the one-and-only, he wanted to help as many people as possible. And given the abundance of need, one man would certainly not be enough. He therefore started to experiment with ways of transferring his healing power to other people. This was how he developed the system of Reiki.

And in doing so broke with Japanese tradition. Enlightenment experiences weren't supposed to be shared (strange as this sounds to a modern ear). In fact, in one of the few texts attributed to Usui, he feels the need to justify his decision. The Japanese original of this text is very old-fashioned and difficult for contemporary Japanese people to understand, and the translation reflects this. However, there is no other commonly accepted translation in circulation.

> *From ancient times whenever someone develops a secret method the one would teach this to the people among family, as a legacy for the later generations of the family living. That idea, not to open to the public and keep that sacred method in the family, is really the past century's bad custom.*
>
> *In modern days we have to live together. That's going to be the basis of happiness, earnestly wanting social progress.*
>
> *That's why I definitely won't allow to keep this for myself.*[2]

The important thing was that Usui's system worked! More and more 'normal' people were attuned and developed healing hands. Interestingly, though, Usui created the opposite of what he'd gone through himself. For me, this is one of the most remarkable aspects of the system! Rather than asking his students to fast and retreat from the world, he developed a system that could be used by anyone in any situation. He must have realized that his harsh mountain retreat was not the only way to make the connection to the universe and that it could be made just as well in normal life.

But how? Usui himself could feel the connection as subtle but intense energetic vibrations. If others could feel the same, he thought, they could gain the same powers. So he felt guided to develop a ritual, now called *Reiju* (in Japanese) or 'attunement' (in the West), which enables everyone to feel this connection in an instant. He added meditation and breathing techniques, suggested hand positions and at some stage introduced symbols as concentration tools for exploring Reiki more deeply. And he asked his students to learn a set of five principles and to reflect on spiritual texts. We will take a more detailed look at the system later (*from page 51*).

Mikao Usui never actually called the *system* Reiki; it is referred to as a system *based on* Reiki. It was simply devised as a way to *connect to* Reiki. In other words, if we want to understand it, we mustn't look at the techniques but at the *source* of the energy.

The training was divided into two levels (Reiki 1 and 2 today) and tailored around the individual student's needs. In terms of income and student numbers, it could be said that Usui's success was moderate. But he persevered, training and treating people, muddling along.

Spreading Reiki

Then disaster struck – and provided another turning-point. This was the earthquake of 1923. Still known as the Great Kanto Earthquake, it was the worst natural disaster in Japanese history up to that time, claiming over 140,000 lives and leaving hundreds of thousands injured. The epicentre lay close to Tokyo and large swathes of the city were destroyed in the ensuing fires.

For months, Usui left his house early in the morning, returned late at night and dedicated his entire time to healing. Faced with the incredible need, he had to come up with new techniques, and is said to have placed one hand on one patient, the other one on a second and even utilized his feet, breath and gaze to transmit Reiki.

He was able to heal an enormous number of people and the disaster provided his breakthrough: afterwards he was known all over Tokyo. He moved to a suburb and opened a new teaching place (*dojo* in Japanese), where he looked after vastly increasing numbers of patients and students.

His students came from all walks of life, but one particular group needs to be singled out: a number of naval officers. They had heard of the success of Usui's method and may have intended to use it in war situations where doctors and medication were out of reach. Their main focus didn't seem to be the spiritual implications – they wanted to learn the healing techniques. Although they could be seen as rather unlikely students, Usui agreed to teach them. Who was he to turn people away? Of course he knew that over time Reiki would open them to a deeper spiritual understanding. And indeed this happened. One of the officers, who composed the text for the memorial stone a few years later, concluded: 'How can [Reiki] be just for curing chronic diseases and longstanding complaints?'[3]

It was this very group that would eventually ensure the continuation of Usui's teachings after his death. Several of them became Reiki teachers (the third and final level that Usui eventually introduced), convinced not only by the effectiveness of the system but also by its simplicity. It may well be that Usui streamlined the system for them and it seems that it was at this stage that what is known today as the Usui system of Reiki was created. Some researchers have suggested that it was also at this point that the now-famous symbols were introduced.

A new system

The memorial makes one thing very clear: Usui's system was entirely new. It was the result of an experience of enlightenment after a long and painful process of self-development. Usui neither rediscovered an ancient system (as is often claimed) nor elaborated on a technique already in use. He simply felt a sudden connection to the universe, an experience of complete oneness, and, to his own surprise, developed healing hands. He then created a system for others also to make, feel and utilize this connection. He may well have been influenced by other techniques and traditions when he was looking for tools to enable his students to access Reiki more deeply, but they weren't the starting-point of the system.

For the author of the memorial stone, this is of such importance that he repeats it several times. I tend to do this, too, as it is such a common misconception that Reiki grew out of existing traditions. Usui himself said, 'Our *Reiki Ryoho* [spiritual energy technique] is a creative idea that no one has developed before and there is nothing like this in this world.'[4]

Palm healing in general, however, was quite popular in Japan during Usui's time. Called *teate* in Japanese, it had been used by the Samurai for centuries and was almost ubiquitous at turn of the nineteenth century. It is still used today. A Japanese student of mine mentioned that her mother used to place her hands on the problem area whenever she suffered from minor ailments like cuts or bruises, headache or fever. The idea behind the practice is that every person can transmit some of their own energy – or *ki* – with healing effects.

But there are two main differences in Usui's method: first (luckily), we don't use our own energy. And secondly, Reiki doesn't just have a soothing effect, but produces the most extraordinary results.

The memorial's author also links the success of the system to Usui's own character: '[His] personality was gentle and modest and he never behaved ostentatiously. ... He was stout-hearted, tolerant and very prudent when undertaking a task.'[5]

Other contemporaries mention that he remained humble and taught with a great sense of humour and compassion. In other words, he taught the way he felt the system should be used: by normal people in everyday life.

On the memorial stone, he is referred to as *Usui-sensei*, which is an honorary way of describing a revered teacher. The somewhat misleading but widely used title of 'doctor' seems to have been added in the 1950s or even later in an attempt to give him more credibility with a Western audience.

Usui's legacy

To reach as many students as possible, Mikao Usui eventually began to travel throughout Japan. He had already suffered two strokes, but carried on regardless, and it was during one of these teaching tours, on 9 March 1926, that he suffered a third stroke and made his transition – in non-Buddhist terms, he died.

Possibly sensing his near passing, only a few weeks before he had gathered the 20 Reiki teachers he had taught (19 were able to attend) and handed each of them an official certificate. As he doesn't seem to have left anything else in writing (at least nothing in the public domain), this was his legacy: 20 men to continue teaching his system of Reiki.

Why did he die so young? After all, Japan tends to top the list of the world's oldest people – and Usui used Reiki every day. So this question is often asked on Reiki courses. It reveals an interesting attitude to age: a long life tends to be associated with a fulfilling one, a short life with tragedy. We often hear that someone died 'too young' or 'before their time'. But really, who are we to know? What was the person meant to learn in this lifetime? What were they here to accomplish? Could this have been achieved in a short life as well?

We will look at these questions in more detail later. Without tackling them, Reiki often doesn't make sense. For now, though, we can certainly come to one conclusion: Usui accomplished quite a bit in his 60 years. Who else has left such a lasting legacy?

Developments after Usui

More information on developments after Usui's death can be found in the appendix (*see page 205*), but for now let's take a brief overview. It is exciting to see how the system survived during tumultuous times.

A teaching organization, the Usui Reiki Ryoho Gakkai, was founded to spread Reiki, and by the mid-1930s it had between 500,000 and 1 million members and branches all over Japan.

One of the founder members, Dr Chujiro Hayashi, left in the 1930s to start a highly successful (and expensive) Reiki clinic in Tokyo. One of his patients recovered from a stomach tumour in 1936 and was so impressed by the treatment that she asked Dr Hayashi to accept her as a student. This lady, an American citizen of Japanese descent called Hawayo Takata (who, as the name suggests, was born and lived in Hawaii), eventually became the first foreign Reiki Master and brought Reiki to the Western world. Over the years, she and the Reiki Masters she trained significantly streamlined the system for the Western audience. By the time of her death in 1980, she'd trained many hundreds of people in Reiki 1 and 2 and taught 22 Reiki Masters. Since then, Reiki has mushroomed all over the globe and it is likely that over 90 per cent of all Reiki students can trace their lineage (*see page 66*) back to one of these 22 teachers.

In the 1990s, though, it came to light that some Japanese Reiki teachers had survived the Second World War and were still using the system, and the Reiki Gakkai, although much diminished, was still operating. So the tradition that was established by Hawayo Takata is now called 'the Western lineage' and the teachings that were preserved in Japan 'the Japanese lineage'. Really they are just two sides of the same coin. But turning it over reveals the true depth of the system.

And that is what I would like to do in this book.

SUMMARY

❖ Prompted by personal disaster, Mikao Usui went on an intense spiritual quest. At the end of it, he reached a moment of enlightenment and obtained healing powers.

❖ He subsequently developed a system and attunement technique that allowed him to pass these abilities on to other people.

❖ The Usui system of Reiki is a unique system not based on any other method or tradition.

Chapter 2

Energy: The universe and the body

Reiki is all about experience. So why do we need to look at science? Well, we don't. The experience and the results are all that matter.

But we humans are a funny species – we have a mind. And this bombards us with questions. *Why* did I just have this experience? *Where* is it coming from? And who knows, we may even attempt to explain Reiki to a sceptical friend. Then science will come in handy.

Nevertheless, I will keep this section as short as I can and limit it to the bare essentials. Because it isn't just about science – it's also about its limitations. For me, this is where it gets even more interesting, for when we reach the boundaries of scientific knowledge, Reiki goes beyond them. And provides a science of its own.

But let's start at the beginning – with energy.

Energy matters

We commonly associate the word 'energy' with higher, finer vibrations. Colour and light, heat and sound are all energy. Or look at your mobile phone. It rings, you answer, and you can talk to a person anywhere in the world without any physical connection.

When we think of energy, we tend to think of these examples. We can't see the energetic vibrations involved, but we can see or hear what they do. And we rightly assume that they must be there.

Then we do the opposite: we see something and know where it is, but we don't see what it does. We call this 'matter'. It is solid, sturdy, reliable. (Interestingly, this judgement even made it into our language: something that *matters* is important.) House, car, cheesecake – all fall into the category of matter.

What is the *connection* between energy and matter? We can see this in action all around us. There might be a tree outside our house, for instance. And a tree (*matter*) needs nourishment to grow: soil, water, sun (*energy*).

This is our comfortable way of perceiving the world. We categorize everything around us; we give it a name. But science tells us differently: *everything* is energy. Sound, light, our heating system ... but also our house, our car and the chair we're sitting on.

Of course, we all learned that at school. We know it in theory. But have we actually internalized it? I certainly haven't! When I see a chair I think of matter. How could something so solid possibly be *energy*? How could a chair vibrate, oscillate, move and change? Well, no matter what I think, it does. It's only because its components vibrate so slowly and at such low frequencies that I perceive it as solid at all.

Our senses simply aren't made to detect these slow movements. I love Einstein's description of matter as 'curdled energy'.

So, the scientific approach to energy can be summed up like this:

❖ Everything is energy. (The entire universe!)

❖ An energy structure is always temporary. (Nothing is ultimately stable – it comes and goes.)

❖ At the smallest – the quantum – level, all energy is the same. (In other words, as there is only one basic ingredient, everything is connected.)

To make it easier, therefore, and more relevant for the understanding of Reiki, we could actually discard the word 'energy' and simply replace it with 'connection' and 'impermanence'.

The physical and the energy body

So often when we look at the world, we see ourselves as slightly detached from it. '*There* is the world. *Here* am I. There is an *outside* (world) and an *inside* (me).' And yet the concept that works for the universe can also be applied to the body. And here it becomes even more interesting.

First, there is *matter*: bones and flesh, blood and organs, all made up of billions of little cells. When we look into a mirror, this is what we see: a body. *Our* body! And of course this is also what we tend to identify with. The body in the mirror is who we are. We take great care of what we see, applying an abundance of creams and lotions to it, going to the gym and eating healthily, and even saying things like 'I'm looking after myself.'

Occasionally, matter – the body, that is – causes problems: parts break, bruise or in various other ways don't function properly. But problems can also be created by other means. Every so often, for instance, we say, 'I have so little energy', 'I feel depleted' or 'I'm exhausted', even though nothing is physically wrong with us. What does this mean?

The obvious: we also have finer, faster vibrations in our body, referred to as 'energy' or 'life-force'. In other languages and traditions this is called *ki*, *chi* or *prana*. And on this basis, an entire library of healing arts has developed, collectively called 'energy healing'. Reiki is often classified as one of them. But is it? Only partially, as we will see.

Becoming aware of the aura

And yet for me it was a complete revelation to see that there was more to us than the physical body – especially as the word 'see' can be taken literally! I'm sure you'll find the following exercise just as fascinating as I do:

Exercise: How to see an aura

❖ Ask another person to stand in front of a plain white or lightly coloured wall, about 30cm (1 ft) away from it.

❖ Stand at least 2–3 metres (6–10 ft) away from the person, then look at the wall around their head or shoulders. (Don't look at the person, otherwise it won't work.)

❖ You may see a strip about 1–2cm (½ in) wide surrounding the body that appears brighter or lighter than the rest. It may be clearly defined by a slim line that looks as though it's been drawn with a pencil. This is a layer of the aura, the energy field of the person.

❖ If you have difficulties detecting the aura, try to soften your gaze a bit. Maybe narrow your eyes a little. Or try a brighter or darker corner of the room.

❖ An alternative method is to spread your fingers against a white or lightly coloured background and look at them. You may detect a slightly blurred but brighter line, this time around 2–3mm (a fraction of an inch) around them.

When we do this exercise on my courses, more than 80 per cent of the students *see* (not just sense) an aura around their fellow students. But even if you can't see an aura at all, let me assure you that you have one. Otherwise it would be a corpse reading this book!

Fascinating though it is, seeing the aura isn't fundamental to learning Reiki. Once we place our hands around a person in a Reiki treatment, we'll become aware of the aura anyway. But it's a fun way to start.

In the exercise we tend to see the innermost layer of the aura, which is one of seven. The further away from the body a layer is, the higher and finer its vibrations. The outermost layer extends to 1–2 metres (around 6 ft) at the front and back of the body, and about half a metre (1½ ft) at the sides. (Just imagine how many people stand in your aura on a packed underground train!) But the aura also changes – and grows with personal development. It seems to follow the equation: small ego = big aura.

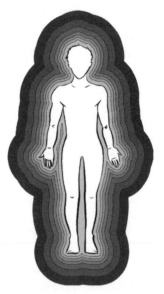

The physical body and the aura

The auric layers surround the physical body in concentric circles, but they also interpenetrate each other, with the innermost being the densest (hence the most easily visible) and the outermost the finest. That means, the vibrational level of the seventh layer surrounds the entire body – and goes through it completely. And what is going on in the aura may eventually manifest in the physical body.

Summing it up, there is certainly more to us than what greets us in the mirror. We are a rather large ball of energy vibrating on various levels and holding plenty of information and potential.

The chakra system

The connection between our energy and our physical body is made through special receptors: the chakras. As over the past decade or two these energy centres have become quite well known, I assume that most readers will be aware that there are seven main chakras located along a central line stretching from the top of the head to the base of the spine.

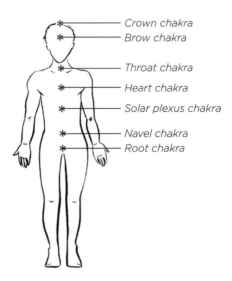

Crown chakra
Brow chakra
Throat chakra
Heart chakra
Solar plexus chakra
Navel chakra
Root chakra

The chakras

Starting from the base, we find the root chakra (at the tail end of the spine), the sacral chakra (about 2cm/1in below the navel) and the solar plexus chakra (at the beginning of the ribcage). Then comes the heart chakra (at the level of the heart but still in the centre of the chest), followed by the throat chakra (around the thyroid), the third eye chakra (the point in between the eyebrows) and the crown chakra (on the top of the head).

Each is connected to the respective layer of the aura – the root chakra with the first, the closest to the physical body, the crown chakra with the seventh, the outermost – and therefore also to the different aspects of our being that they represent. Now this whole concept becomes a science: the innermost layer is mainly concerned with aspects of our physical incarnation, the outermost with our spiritual connection, and the ones in between with various other aspects of our being. It is as fascinating as it is complex.

And much of it makes great sense. A blockage around the throat chakra may have to do with a lack of communication (for example, we should be having a proper conversation with our boss or spouse and not keeping our unhappiness inside), the heart chakra deals with relationships and empathy, the solar plexus with our inner strength, the navel chakra with emotions, the root chakra keeps us grounded, the third eye opens our intuition and the crown chakra helps us to realize our connection to the divine.

The chakras are also connected to the surrounding physical areas: the heart chakra (obviously) to the heart, the sacral chakra to the stomach and small intestines, and so on. In practice, this means that a blockage around the throat chakra could still be caused by a communication issue, but also by a sore throat or a stiff neck. Or, in fact, the sore throat itself could be caused by a communication problem...

Traditionally, the chakras and their respective auric layers are shown in certain colours – the root red, sacral orange, solar plexus yellow, heart green, throat blue, third eye indigo and crown purple – and it is indeed possible to become aware of these colours when dealing with a particular chakra. During a Reiki attunement, many students see some of these colours, most notably purple or green.

The energy, or *ki*, brought in through the chakras is transported around the body through an enormous number of *meridians* and *nadis*, which are something like energy arteries and veins. The first are larger, the latter smaller, and some ancient charts show 72,000 of them. Without detailed knowledge of their location, a therapy like acupuncture wouldn't even be thinkable. When performing open-heart surgery without anaesthesia, aided only by a few long needles, you need to be fairly confident about the correct positioning!

There are many good books detailing the chakra system and its connection to mind, body and spirit. Elements of it are also taught on most Reiki courses – after all, it's great to become more aware of the subtleties of our existence on Earth. And yet when it comes to Reiki, we face a surprise: this knowledge is *not* a prerequisite for its use. It is helpful and interesting – but not necessary. Reiki will guide the practitioner. It is simply impossible to place the hands wrongly! Even if, for some reason, it's impossible to get close to the location of the physical problem, Reiki will get there anyway, as scores of Reiki recipients have experienced.

Carol, a Reiki 1 student, was completely bewildered after her first treatment. Her fellow student had placed their hands only around her head, but she'd felt a sensation in her left knee. The whole group was stunned when she revealed that she'd had botched surgery there.

With this in mind, it will be less of a surprise to learn that the chakra system was neither widely known in Japan in the early twentieth century nor taught by Mikao Usui. Instead, Reiki offers an alternative concept that explains not just the flow of *ki* but also our entire human existence and its relationship to the universe. This isn't meant to replace the chakra system – in fact, it complements this understanding perfectly – but it goes even deeper.

The universe according to Reiki

The level of form

In the philosophy of Reiki we still find the duality of energy and matter, but here they are still part of the *same* experience: our earthly existence. As we saw above, even on a mechanical level we can only function when we have the correct combination of both. Energy and matter together create our experience of life on the level of form – that is, on *Earth*. Utilizing a Taoist concept, Mikao Usui therefore called this *Earth energy*.

Earth energy includes everything we need to exist on this level: food and shelter, body and clothing, income and work. Without these, life is rather difficult. We have incarnated on planet Earth and this set-up comes with needs. When resources are scarce, trouble looms: we find ourselves hungry or homeless, sick or cold, poor or unemployed. In fact, most of the time there's something in our life that isn't perfect. Our food isn't healthy or our house too small; we aren't well or our clothes aren't the latest fashion; our income isn't sufficient or we hate our job.

Of course, in all these cases we're looking for change – change for the better. Physical healing, a new job, a loving partner – or just a slightly easier life! I'm sure I'm not far off in suggesting that in one way or another almost everybody is looking for change. Reiki can help with all of this.

In the system of Reiki, Earth energy is represented by the *Power Symbol*. (*For more on this, see page 158.*) This helps to bring the power of Reiki into the here and now. Or, to stay in the wording, to bring it down to *Earth*.

The level of spirit

But, contrary to what we are often given to believe in our science lessons, the level of form (the Earth and other planets and stars) isn't the *entire* universe. Where were we before we were born? Where are we going back to? There is a world beyond this one.

This other level of the universe is the *spirit realm*. Here we find guides, angels and bodhisattvas and all the people who are in between incarnations. We are well known to those in this world and have lots of friends there – unlike, as it often turns out, on Earth.

This 'parallel world' is constantly present and when we raise our vibrations (or the guys up there lower theirs), we can get in contact with it. Then we can receive guidance, support and insight – or maybe just feel a presence.

New ideas and creativity, harmony and balance are the result of this connection, which Mikao Usui aptly called *Heaven energy*. Not in the sense that this is paradise (although it probably feels like it compared with our experience on Earth), but in the sense of being the unseen, the before-and-after. A higher realm, with lighter, finer vibrations. Something *above*.

To deepen our awareness of our connection to the spirit realm and therefore enable us to open up to guidance and intuition and finding more harmony and balance in life, Usui introduced the *Harmony Symbol* (*see page 161*).

Interconnectedness

Contrary to outer appearance, nothing on either the level of form or the level of spirit operates independently. On the level of form, everything is ultimately connected (see quantum physics) and it's the same on the level of spirit (after all, everything there is still energy, as many reports from that realm show). And, as we have just seen, the two levels are themselves closely entwined.

Individually, we may consider ourselves to be a lonely being floating around in the universe. But this is an illusion. Whether we like it or not, we're connected to the entire world. Which, of course, brings responsibilities. Everything we do has an effect on others.

We are now tapping into the idea of *oneness* – and getting much closer to the heart of Reiki. This is what Reiki does: it brings us closer. To other humans, to other beings, to nature, to meaning, to ourselves. And, typically, it gets practical: Reiki *utilizes* this concept. Every Reiki treatment is proof that we are connecting with a person on a deeper level, even if we keep our hands away from them. A particularly spectacular result of this 'applied oneness' is the ability to send Reiki over vast distances (*see page 113*).

To help his students concentrate on connection, and ultimately oneness, Mikao Usui created the *Connection Symbol* (*see page 164*).

The body according to Reiki

Now we'll move on and look at the body in a slightly different way. We'll take the Reiki view and see the body as a universe in itself. And what a revelation this was for me!

The three *Tanden* points

There are three main energy centres along our body, called *Tanden* points in Japanese (or *Dantien* in Chinese). They reflect the structure of the universe (*see image overleaf*).

The lower *Tanden*: Earth energy

The first is called *Hara*, or *lower Tanden*. This is our point of connection with *Earth energy*. It represents our existence in the here and now.

It is also the location of the energy (*ki*) of the body. From it, *ki* moves up the central meridian (also called *Hara*) and is distributed throughout the body.

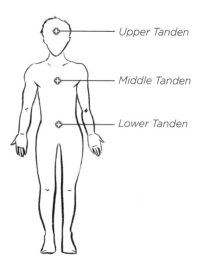

The Tanden *points*

When we store and maintain enough *ki* in this point, we are strong and healthy and can deal with the demands of the level of form.

This *Tanden* is also the centre of the body in terms of steadiness. Sumo wrestlers can consolidate their strength there so that they're almost invincible. Only when they are distracted can they be toppled. Focusing on the *Hara* is the key.

The upper *Tanden*: heaven energy

Then we move to the obvious opposite of Earth: *heaven*. Our connection to heaven energy lies around the brow chakra, often called the *third eye*.

Most people are aware of this point through seeing Indian people sporting a dot there. Not too many observers tend to know, though, that this isn't meant to be merely a pretty adornment. It is supposed to remind the wearer that they don't just have two physical eyes to see the outer world but also a 'third eye' to see and sense intuitively.

When opening up spiritually, people often feel sensations at this point. In India, some people put sandalwood paste there to cool it down.

The duality of heaven and Earth energy is often felt in an attunement. We feel the movement of energy, often as a sensation in our palms, and may also experience a strong sensation between the eyebrows.

The middle *Tanden*: experience of oneness
In the middle between heaven and Earth we find another energy centre: the heart chakra or third *Tanden* point.

This is the point from which we reach out to others – the point of empathy and love. And it is here of course that we can feel love physically. Don't we get a feeling of warmth in our chest when we're in love? When we're in love with someone, we feel close to them, we want to be with them, we open up to them, we want to share, to know more. We strive to become one with them.

We naturally have feelings of love and connection. Mother Teresa probably had them in abundance, many people retrieve them when prompted, and with some people they're buried so deeply that they only come out when they pat their dog. But the feeling of oneness is there nevertheless – and sharing Reiki is based on it.

A mirror of the universe

In essence, all this means that our body is a microcosm. Anything that can be experienced *outside* can also be experienced *inside*. The question is: are we a mirror of the universe – or is the universe a mirror of us?

The answer is neither. It is simply the same experience. Because we're all connected.

In some Eastern traditions, the *Tanden* points are called the *Three Diamonds*. Once they are properly polished, they reveal their beauty, their shine and their sparkle. And this is our task...

Beyond energy

Having explored the elements of the universe, we may wonder, *Is that all?* Or is there something *beyond* the universe? In other words, beyond *energy*?

Science has established that the world is in constant change. Which in turn leads to the questions: does energy change *by itself*? Is there intelligence *in* energy? Or is energy simply the base material used *by* intelligence? Food for thought...

Ki, Rei and *Reiki*

So how does Reiki fit in? Isn't it an 'energy-healing modality'? I place this in inverted commas because it really is a lot more than that. It brings everything together – heaven and Earth.

The word *Reiki* is made up of the phonetics of two Japanese *kanji*. *Kanji* are logographic characters, something like an alphabet but made up of syllables or short words rather than letters. Each *kanji* already has a meaning in itself, but the combination of two or more can lead to an entirely different meaning. To make things easier, with the word *Reiki* this is not the case – its meaning is simply the result of the two *kanji* that form it. So we can start by looking at them individually.

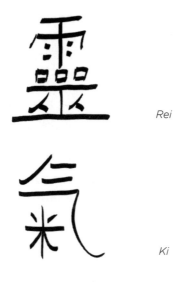

Rei

Ki

Reiki in Japanese writing

Ki

The easier *kanji* to explore is certainly the second one: *ki*.

The idea of *ki* can be found in almost every Eastern spiritual system. In fact it can be found in almost every Eastern understanding of the world. Called *chi* or *qi* in Chinese (but using the same symbol as in Japanese, as the word was imported into Japanese around AD800), or *prana* in

Sanskrit (the ancient language of the Indian subcontinent), it probably has been around forever. It is mentioned in the *Vedas*, said to be the oldest written texts in the world.

The meaning is always the same: 'the energy that animates the world'. According to Wikipedia,[1] the ancient Chinese believed it 'permeated everything and linked their surroundings together'. Variously translated as 'universal energy', 'life energy' or 'life-force energy', it is supposed to be present in every living being in the universe. The more strongly it is felt, the better the flow, and the stronger and healthier the life-form.

You may wonder why we don't have a similar expression in Western philosophy. Well, we used to: ancient Greek and Egyptian philosophy, as well as many shamanic traditions, incorporated the idea of energy flowing through every living being, but it somehow got lost a few thousand years ago. However, it has started to re-emerge with the more holistic worldview of recent times.

In short, *ki* means 'life energy'. If there is no *ki*, there is no life. *Ki* powers the universe. It is in every living being and is always the same. When condensed, it creates life; when diluted, it just permeates everything.

In the older forms of the Japanese *kanji* (*see page 37*), *ki* is depicted as an asterix, which stands for a grain of rice. The staple food of the East (the Chinese are reported to say that if they have not had rice during the day *they have not eaten*), it represents the key ingredient needed to sustain life. The lines on top represent the aura (literally 'ether') of the rice grain. They seem to say that there is more to the rice than we can see.

The contemporary *kanji* uses a simplified version, an 'x', but basically it means the same.

Rei

Rei can be translated as 'universal', 'divine', 'essence', 'spirit' or simply 'God'. But looking at its pictogram can reveal its practical relevance.

As you can see, the upper part of the pictogram looks like rain. And that is exactly what it means: it is raining down from heaven, i.e. heaven is opening up, bringing us nourishment.

But it doesn't come down automatically – we need to ask for it! That is what the bottom part of the pictogram represents: a *miko*, that is, a priest, shaman or wise person. In other words, a person who knows how to get in contact with the 'above'.

The older form of *kanji* (*see page 37*) also includes an element that has been left out of newer versions: a row of three containers (or 'mouths'). Again, this is to be taken literally: what comes from above can be collected in the three containers (or energy centres) in our body, the *Tanden* points – the *Hara*, third eye and heart chakra.

Reiki

In the Western tradition, the word *Reiki* is often translated as 'universal life-force energy'. But, as we have just seen, this falls short of its full meaning, as it mainly translates the *ki* aspect. Playing with words, it can be said that the *ki* aspect is not the key aspect. The key to Reiki is understanding its higher connection. The best translation, therefore, would be 'spiritual energy'. Or even 'spiritually guided energy'.

Put simply, *Reiki* means 'heaven and Earth coming together'. Or, if we want to keep the word 'universal', we could say 'the energy of oneness'. We are connecting to the entire universe – and its creator. Personally, I tend to just use the translation of 'universal energy'. It implies all the above.

SUMMARY

✦ Science has revealed that everything is energy. On the quantum level, everything is the same – and therefore interconnected.

✦ The three levels of existence in the universe – form (Earth energy), spirit (heaven energy) and interconnectedness (oneness) – are reflected in the three *Tanden* points (energy centres) in our body.

✦ *Reiki* means 'heaven and Earth coming together'.

Chapter 3
Healing: Our body and our life

Yes, Reiki can heal! There is an abundance of proof. Doctors at the Charité, Berlin's University Hospital, for instance, concluded a few years ago that complementary therapies could speed up healing time, reduce the need for painkillers and generally improve the wellbeing of patients. (They could probably cut costs too, as patients could vacate their hospital beds earlier.) Unsure which therapy to go for, the doctors trialled a number of them and analysed the patient feedback. With 85 per cent of patients reporting a reduction in pain, Reiki scored the highest by far. Today, the hospital runs a specialist Reiki department with five permanent staff.[1] The results are extraordinary.

Many health organizations now acknowledge the benefits of Reiki. Treatment (often provided by volunteers) is offered in many hospitals in the UK and the USA. A number of clinical trials have demonstrated its benefits, including a reduction in the side effects of cancer treatments like chemotherapy and radiotherapy.

And of course there are the reports from numerous individuals about how they have benefited from Reiki. Take Alistair, for instance, a student of mine who suffered from heart palpitations. He first came across Reiki on the internet. A practitioner had advertised free distance treatments to people in need. (What a wonderful idea!) Alistair got in touch and, as he was an accountant by training, kept a meticulous journal of his palpitations. After a few weeks of Reiki, he found occurrences had reduced from 28 times to three or four times a month. And of course he's no exception. There is so much evidence that Reiki works.

In scientific terms, reports like Alistair's are categorized as *anecdotal* evidence. An anecdote is an individual experience. With Reiki, however, we have *millions* of such anecdotes. And many report very similar results. That means the anecdotal becomes *empirical*. Quantifiable. Measurable. Hence scientific.

So, there is scientific proof that Reiki works. And yet, despite many theories, there's no simple scientific explanation of *how* it works. When we look at the results, the reason for that becomes clearer: it doesn't work in one way but many. Just as we humans can be quite complex...

The concept of holistic healing

I am very grateful to Reiki teacher Penelope Quest for introducing me to the concept of *holistic healing*. In other words, not just looking at the body but at the whole person. Working holistically means we don't just focus on a symptom but take into account cause and effect. After all, if we treat the symptom and not the cause, it will inevitably reappear.

Healing on different levels

With regards to Reiki, four levels of healing are commonly distinguished:

1. *Physical:* Anything to do with the body (our own and those of others).

2. *Emotional:* How we react to and deal with our experiences (both consciously and subconsciously).

3. *Mental:* Our attitudes and thought patterns (decisions, directions and lifestyle choices).

4. *Spiritual:* The bigger picture (finding meaning, acceptance and – possibly the most difficult thing of all – forgiveness).

I would like to add a fifth (very practical) level: *life circumstances* (through unexpected changes or out-of-the-blue encounters, often summed up as synchronicity).

In many, if not most, cases, the levels are interconnected. For instance, a physical problem (a painful knee) may have been caused by another physical problem (a twisted ankle that affected the balance of the knee). Physical problems can also affect our emotions (I am depressed because my painful knee keeps me from taking a walk in the sunshine) or vice versa (I am sad and my body posture reflects this, leading to tension and headaches). The body–mind connection has been the subject of much research recently, including into the healing effects of positive thinking and the dangerous effects of stress.

For Reiki, this means there's often more behind a symptom than meets the eye and we need to stay open to the possibility of healing on more than one level.

This happened to my student Dee, who treated a lady for a frozen shoulder. She was one of her first clients and Dee was full of anticipation. She was hoping to cure the pain, but nothing happened. Instead, during the treatment her client found herself constantly thinking about money. In the subsequent conversation, it emerged that she was self-employed and was deeply worried about the lack of work coming in.

A few weeks later they met again and the client reported a great surge in jobs and therefore in money coming in. The frozen shoulder had been a sign of 'shouldering' all this responsibility for her family! And of course the symptoms then eased too.

The cough story

Let's take a little challenge. Say someone suffers from a cough, goes to the doctor, gets a prescription of antibiotics and painkillers and takes a few days off work. The cough eventually disappears. Person healed, case closed. This is the classic approach of Western medicine: you diagnose what is physically wrong with a person, find a cure (chemical substances, new technologies, often surgery) and the symptoms leave the body. The person is healed.

But are they really? Of course they aren't coughing at present. Is this healing? Let's look into this a little more deeply.

What if the cough comes back a few weeks later? You may say, 'That person was unlucky to catch a cough twice in a short time.' But what if the person didn't actually 'catch' the cough? The cough may be a consequence of their lifestyle: not eating healthily, not getting enough vitamin C, smoking, not sleeping enough, getting stressed at work or at home, worrying, venting anger, not exercising or not getting enough fresh air. What if they live in a damp flat? Or work in an environment where chemicals are used or dust is produced? Does healing then lie in curing the symptom temporarily or in a change of circumstances?

Imagine the person actually *wants* to have a cough. (This is possible, though the decision would be likely to be made subconsciously, rather than as a result of logical thinking.) They *want* to be a patient. *Want* to be cared for. *Want* to be pitied. *Want* to be the centre of attention. They may feel this is the only way to get attention and love. Or they may be – consciously or subconsciously – looking for an excuse not to work. Not to shoulder responsibility. Not to communicate with people by whom they feel threatened. Does healing then lie in curing the symptom or in listening and accepting and showing love and affection?

Let's look more deeply now... What if none of the above applies – and the cough still keeps coming back? Or just stays? What if tons of antibiotics can't get rid of it? What if the person has a mental or emotional problem and doesn't know how to deal with it? Could the cough be the only thing the body can come up with in its attempt to rid the person of it? Where would healing start then? Maybe in a long conversation? In providing an open and understanding environment?

We can look even more deeply. What if the patient had a cough in their childhood during a phase when they suffered problems at school and abuse at home? Could the persistence of the cough be a sign that the emotional scars haven't yet healed? Is the cough a sign of the trauma hidden inside?

And let's take one last look. Imagine the person has died from tuberculosis in a previous life, lived in a damp and cold refugee camp or been a medieval prisoner of war...

A cough may be a simple example. But it proves how deeply we might have to investigate. And how far off we can be when just treating the symptoms. Reiki often leads us to discover the root of a problem (*see page 174*). And the healing journey can take a turn for the unexpected.

The school of life

There's a strange thing about healing, no matter which therapy we use: it never works completely. Of course, if we have a broken leg, it may get fixed and heal, and after a few weeks be perfectly usable again. But that won't prevent us from breaking an arm a while later. Or losing our job. Or going through a painful divorce. And even if we're having a relatively easy time in our own life, we just need to watch the news to destroy our sense of happiness. Only this morning I heard that some debris from a plane has been found in the sea near Borneo. All 162 passengers are dead. How can I be happy if others aren't?

Life is never free of problems. It almost seems to be *designed* to have them. But why? Is there meaning behind it all?

I believe there is. And the meaning is: learning. Every time we encounter a problem, we are prompted to rethink. We reflect – and often change. We change our lifestyle, our thought patterns, our path...

Of course it's much more pleasant not to experience problems in the first place. But if we look back honestly, would we be where we are today if we hadn't gone through challenging times?

I find it helpful sometimes to take a moment, look back and ask myself: 'Have you learned from the difficult times?' If I could turn the clock back, would I really want to avoid all my problems? I wanted to avoid them when I was right in the middle of them, of course. And quite a few of those difficulties are still so traumatic (or embarrassing) that I would rather erase them from my memory altogether. But I'm sure they all served their purpose. Even though some just make me think: *Never again.*

Some (rather advanced) people even look at an illness or a problem in a positive way: 'What a chance for me to develop! Maybe that illness was much needed! Maybe true healing lies in acceptance rather than curing.'

In terms of Reiki, this means a result may not always be exactly what we expect or hope for. After all, do we really know what we're supposed to learn in this life? If there wasn't a lesson waiting for us here, I suppose there wouldn't have been much reason to incarnate in the first place. After all, the spirit realm seems to be a much nicer place to stay.

When we look at the Buddhist influences on Reiki, of course the idea of reincarnation comes to mind. Once we consider this lifetime as just one of many, we tend to get less attached to it. And find it easier to see life as a learning opportunity. (Incidentally, the concept of reincarnation isn't exclusive to Buddhism; it has been part of many religions – including Christianity for the first 500 years of its existence. In the middle of the sixth century, the Second Council of Constantinople erased all references to it from the Bible.)

Healing and wholing

So, there is healing, and there is learning. And the two are somewhat connected. Reiki works for both: it brings healing in very practical ways and also makes us more aware of the path of learning that we follow. As millions of 'users' all over the world have testified, we become healthier and happier as a result of Reiki, and often see our life path more clearly. Even large steps may be taken: we learn the qualities of patience or love, compassion or acceptance. Or whatever our incarnation is supposed to focus on.

Often we feel more 'whole'. Because healing, ultimately, is *wholing*. 'To heal' comes from the same source as 'to become whole'. And, as so often, the meaning unfolds on different levels. As we explored in the last chapter, there is the physical body – and it only functions properly when we look after all its parts. Then there is the energy body – and the two are interconnected. We move from body to person, and now include mental and emotional aspects, attitudes and feelings. Our thoughts, our mind, can majorly influence our physical and energy body. And we become aware of intuition and guidance, and realize that we are somehow connected to the spirit realm. We are both body and spirit. Or, in Reiki terms, heaven and Earth energy, connected to the entire universe. We may (at least in theory) realize that we are connected to every other being. That the whole universe is one.

And yet, this is *not* being whole. It simply describes the set-up of the universe. We may feel one with everything yet still wonder what it's all about. After all, we are also one with sorrow and tragedy. Oneness therefore means having compassion – and sharing other people's problems. But is this enough ultimately to heal us?

I think the following example shows what becoming whole really means. One of my first students came to Reiki to find relief for his back problems. He'd damaged his spine a few years earlier, without noticing straight away. His back had got worse and worse and eventually a disc needed to be replaced by a metal tube. The wound had not healed as well as hoped and he'd been in great pain and off work for several months. Which was when he decided to join a Reiki course.

On the course, when I talked about the messages an illness could have, he started to reflect. For the rest of the weekend he pondered over what he was meant to *learn* from his condition and how he was meant to *change*. And after a while, the symptoms started to ease.

By the time he came on the Reiki 2 course, he'd gone beyond change and entered a phase of realization. His main comment was: 'No matter what happens, the problems are *just in my body* – they don't affect who I really am.'

Healing had become *spiritual awakening*. And he'd started to become aware of the ultimate lesson: realizing who we really are. We can only be whole when we find this truth.

And what a lesson for me: he'd become a Reiki Master without taking the Master-level course!

Awakening isn't about taking a course. It can happen at any moment.

This student had realized that healing wasn't to be found in change but in the unchangeable. He'd had a glimpse of a presence – of the eternal *now* – and realized that this was beyond the universe we live in.

This is all pretty deep. Don't be concerned – Reiki can be used to most wonderful effect without any of these considerations. But you may find that at some stage some of these deeper questions will arise. Then it will be helpful to find that Reiki can provide so many answers. After all, Mikao Usui never looked for physical healing to start with. His quest was to uncover the connection to the *unchangeable*. He was just as surprised as every Reiki student today when he suddenly found himself with healing hands. The heart of his teachings was using Reiki for spiritual development.

SUMMARY

* There is abundant empirical proof that Reiki brings measurable healing.

* Reiki not only heals on several levels – physical, mental, emotional and spiritual – but also assists with life circumstances.

* Healing and personal development cannot be separated.

Part II
THE SYSTEM
OF REIKI

'The only source of knowledge is experience.'
ALBERT EINSTEIN

Chapter 4

An overview of the system of Reiki

Now that we have 'the basics' in place, we are finally able to take a detailed look at the original system of Reiki.

The elements of the system:

1. *Attunements:* To open and deepen our individual connection to Reiki.

2. *Palm-healing techniques:* To enable us to give Reiki treatments.

3. *Breathing, cleansing and meditation techniques:* To clear any blockages between us and Reiki.

4. *Symbols and mantras:* To bring us a deeper awareness of the universe and our place in it.

5. *Principles and poetry:* To enable us to reflect on our attitudes and conduct.

All these elements can be found at every level of Reiki teachings. As we deepen our connection to Reiki, we will also deepen our understanding of them.

How Reiki is taught

Traditionally, Reiki is taught on three levels. However, in some Japanese traditions the second and third levels are subdivided into two tiers each. (Nothing additional is normally taught – only the learning time extended.) Mikao Usui seems to have often customized his teaching to meet the individual requirements of his students. So it may have ranged from a crash course (two levels over four or five consecutive days) to an extended training programme of several months.

This, though, is the general format:

Level 1

Western name: Reiki 1

Japanese name: Shoden (the beginner's teachings)

Prerequisites: Absolutely none. Just turn up.

It includes:

❖ attunements (normally four)

❖ basic palm-healing techniques

❖ breathing, cleansing and meditation techniques

❖ the Reiki principles

❖ symbols and mantras (albeit only implicitly: they are used by the teacher during the attunements but are not revealed to the students)

Level 2

Western name: Reiki 2

Japanese name: Okuden (the deeper/inner teachings)

Prerequisites: Reiki 1 (and ideally a few weeks or months of practice, but this is not absolutely essential)

It includes:

❖ attunements (normally one, but sometimes up to three)

❖ advanced and more intuitive palm-healing techniques

❖ more breathing and meditation

❖ a deeper look at the principles

❖ three symbols and mantras (the Power, Harmony and Connection Symbols)

❖ the requirements for practising Reiki professionally (included on some Western-style courses only)

Level 3

Western name: Master/Teacher level

Japanese name: Shinpiden (the mystery teachings) or *Shihan* (Teacher)

Prerequisites: Reiki 1 and 2 and some experience as a practitioner. Some teachers ask for a minimum period of one or two years between Reiki 2 and Reiki Master level.

It includes:

❖ a Master attunement (normally one, but sometimes two)

- even more breathing and meditation

- the Master symbol and mantra

- a deeper look at all teachings from previous levels

- how to give attunements/*Reiju*

- how to teach Reiki

Philosophy

Moving away from the technical aspects, we can also look at the structure in a philosophical way:

- Reiki 1 (*Shoden*), the beginner's level, is about physical healing and opening up to guidance from the universe.

- Reiki 2 (*Okuden*), the deeper teachings, explains our connection to the universe.

- The Master level (*Shinpiden*), the mystery teachings, looks at the existential questions. Why are we here? What are we connected to? Where are we coming from? Or simply: Who am I?

Prerequisites

There are no prerequisites for learning Reiki. No particular abilities, no particular personal characteristics are required. No belief in it either! I once had a student who only came to silence her best friend, who had been telling her to learn Reiki for years. She only enrolled on the course 'to have proof once and for all that Reiki is rubbish' (this is the expression she used). And yet I have rarely had such a dedicated Reiki student. Two years later she was a Reiki Master and had built an astonishingly successful Reiki practice. She credits Reiki with transforming her life – and her whole family agrees.

I tend to find that Reiki comes into our life when it is the right moment for it. So if you feel like learning Reiki, just start. You will be ready, no matter whether you have meditated for the past 10 years or are going through a crisis and feel all over the place.

Disabilities aren't a problem, either. Reiki can be practised in many creative ways. Not even hands are ultimately needed.

Finding a Reiki teacher

The easiest way to find the right teacher is to ask the universe for guidance. You may find that you meet someone in the unlikeliest of places (someone came on a Master course with me after we met on a beach in Spain) or simply Google for one. If you feel attracted to a certain website, name or photo, then this person is likely to be the right one to start with. (It's perfectly fine to train with somebody else for the next level.)

Every teacher has their own style, personality and experiences. The main criteria for me is dedication. I would be a bit careful if a teacher offered 20-odd other disciplines as well. Reiki should be the main focus. Also, I would make sure that it was Usui Reiki that was being taught, not another discipline that had borrowed the name (*see page 213*).

Asking questions

Once you are on a course, don't take everything at face value. If something doesn't make sense to you, ask the teacher for further explanation. There are no stupid questions, only stupid answers. Mikao Usui was bombarded with questions in his courses and answered them all patiently and happily. Of course, a teacher may not always have the exact answer, but they can point you in the right direction.

The duration of a course

The core curriculum for Reiki in the UK states that Reiki 1 and 2 should be taught over a minimum of 12 hours each – for example, a weekend course or four half-days. This allows enough time for the body to adjust to the energy and for the student to gain practical experience, look at the history and philosophy of Reiki and discuss any questions. An afternoon, or even a day, is simply not enough. And certainly doesn't do Reiki justice. Also, for professional accreditation, these short formats are not accepted.

The Master training can have a variety of formats. We will discuss the options in Chapter 10.

SUMMARY

❖   The elements of the system of Reiki are: attunements; palm healing; breathing, cleansing; meditation; symbols and mantras; principles and poetry.

❖   Reiki is traditionally taught on three levels.

❖   No prerequisites are needed – everyone can learn Reiki.

Chapter 5

Attunements:
Finding the light switch

An attunement is the one element that sets Reiki apart from any other therapy – as well as from most spiritual disciplines. It is a ritual (or initiation) that not only creates a connection to Reiki for each recipient, but also guarantees that this connection is always the same. It is the only indispensable element of Reiki. Everything else is a non-essential addition.

Reiki is often called *light healing* – and an attunement enables us to feel the light within. In essence this means Reiki starts with a moment of enlightenment. Always. For everyone. Guaranteed. No matter whether a student is aware of it or not.

How it works

Healing hands were the result of Mikao Usui's moment of enlightenment. After three weeks of meditation on Mount Kurama, he literally 'saw the light'. In his own words, it was 'almost blindingly bright'. At that moment he felt complete oneness with the universe and directly connected to its divine source.

Going beyond the ego (something that the many semi-enlightened people around today still have to learn), he didn't want to keep the light for himself. As we learned earlier, in his humility he was convinced that he couldn't possibly be the only one – or one of only a few – to make this inner connection. What worked for him would surely work for others.

Luckily for us, he didn't demand of his students the same rigid discipline he had gone through. He didn't want to create any more suffering, he only wanted to share light and love – the light and love he could feel inside through his connection to Reiki.

He developed a technique to establish such a deep connection to his students that they could actually feel Reiki flowing through him. When he set his intention to share his Reiki connection with them, he found they were able to make that connection subsequently themselves.

This is exactly what we do today.

There are several attunement techniques, but they all seem to bring the same result. (Which confirms once again that the key to Reiki is never the technique. Reiki is always about the *experience*, about the *connection*.) Japanese traditions concentrate more on the idea of 'bringing down energy from the universe' and making it accessible, whereas Western techniques tend to utilize the Reiki symbols. Japanese versions are called *Reiju* ('spiritual blessing') and tend to be shorter but repeated more often; Western versions are called *attunements* (literally *aligning* to universal energy).

Both are merely concentration aids for the Reiki teacher, helping them to focus on the depth of Reiki and enable the student to feel it.

In both traditions, the students are asked to close their eyes (to concentrate better and 'listen inside') and, at some point, bring their hands together in *Gassho*, the prayer position (*see page 126*). Moving around each student, the teacher then places their hands on or near the student's body in several positions. At some stage they place their hands around those of the student to 'open' their palms for healing.

A good analogy is an old-fashioned radio: the technical essentials are all in place but the aerial needs to be adjusted to pick up the signal. Once this is done, we can hear the music more clearly, and after some fine-tuning, the connection is perfect.

As listed earlier, the Reiki 1 course normally has four attunements and Reiki 2 and the Master level have one each, although again there are variations. Technically, it isn't necessary to give four attunements in Reiki 1, but the idea is gradually to open the channel in the student over the course of just two days. In the UK, the guidelines for Reiki teaching (agreed by all main Reiki Associations under the umbrella of the Reiki Council) list four Reiki 1 attunements as a general requirement.

Experiences and effects

Experiences

When I had my first attunement I was pretty unaware of all this. I was definitely unaware of the idea of enlightenment.

But then, I wasn't aware of anything: I felt absolutely nothing throughout the entire process. My first reaction was: 'That's typical! These things never work for me!' Half an hour later I started to feel a strange tingling in my palms. Healing hands were arriving.

My experience (or rather non-experience) is one end of the spectrum. A student of mine summed up the other. Speechless for quite a while after her attunement, she eventually said, 'I saw God.' I still remember the expression on her face – a combination of complete happiness and utter disbelief.

She is not the only student who has felt a deep connection to their religious belief during an attunement. Some feel the presence of Jesus, others the Prophet Mohammed. Some encounter angels.

Many others experience the unexpected in less obvious terms: they see colours (often purple or green) through closed eyes, forming amorphous shapes that move like those in lava lamps. Others feel lightness in their body (like floating) or heaviness in their hands (like being given something), or localized sensations of heat, cold or energy movement.

Some even feel a slight temporary pain, others the easing of a physical problem. Many feel emotional and have a sense of peace, calm and belonging. The majority use terms like 'weird' or 'strange' to describe their experiences. They are different from anything they have come across before and often leave them rather puzzled.

An attunement is a very profound experience and I will therefore try to make some more sense of what we may perceive during one. The experiences tend to fall into three main categories:

1. Clearing blockages for the flow of Reiki
Meridians and chakras are opened, blockages are cleared and energy flows more freely. In the body, this is felt as hot or cold sensations, sudden body movements and more sensitivity on one side of the body than on the other. Occasionally, slight headaches or pain in other areas are felt, the hands get heavy and the feet get warm. The experiences are often particularly localized.

2. Stirring up emotions
Feelings of happiness or sadness come up, flashbacks occur and memories surface. We may feel rather overwhelmed and confused.

3. Opening to spiritual realms
Experiences of floating or light-headedness are common. We may feel a presence (angels, guides, family members in the spirit world), sense light or colours and have an overall sense of love and gratitude. We feel a connection to something deeper and an inner vastness.

Something is happening
All these experiences have one thing in common: something is *happening*. They are neither anticipated nor imagined. To our surprise, they are just there. Reiki starts to flow, blockages to clear, and we begin to sense our connection to levels we may not have thought existed.

Many of these experiences will reappear when we give or receive Reiki treatments. (*See page 96 for a long list of the potential experiences and effects that Reiki can bring.*)

No matter exactly what we experience, and no matter how intense, subtle or even uneventful it might be, a Reiki attunement always works. The door to Reiki is always opened.

Effects

The effects of an attunement can also be summarized in three categories:

1. Inner connection

An inner connection to Reiki is opened – for the rest of our life. It will deepen with regular use. But don't worry if you haven't used Reiki for a while. Even if you haven't practised it for many years and then suddenly feel that it might come in handy, just think of it and it will be there. It may lie dormant, but it can always be called upon.

2. Healing hands and intuition

Soon after the attunement, a sensation tends to arrive in our hands. For many, it is felt as unusual warmth; for others, tingling or pulsating. Some people feel little themselves and only become aware that they have healing hands through the feedback they get when they place them on another person.

Occasionally Reiki may 'switch itself on' after an attunement. You may be sitting on the underground and suddenly feel an intense heat where your hands are resting on your lap.

There's nothing to worry about – just enjoy what's going on. You obviously need Reiki at that moment.

Many students are surprised by how their intuitive abilities increase. They become more aware of other people's feelings and may even sense future events. They are tapping into the interconnectedness of the universe.

3. A 21-day clearing process
An attunement starts an inner process of cleansing that is often most noticeable over the first three weeks (and hence called the 21-day clearing process). In some cases it may last as long as a few months, in many others just a week. It is a proper inner decluttering, but may vary in intensity. Many students need to use the toilet more often (flushing out toxins), others completely relive their lives, experiencing thoughts, behavioural patterns, dreams and memories that often are as toxic as chemicals. But they can now deal with them.

We might think of this as a process of physical, mental, emotional and spiritual transformation. I have had students who have given up smoking or drinking, changed partner or job, or found their attitude towards life has changed completely after an attunement. Others have felt little, if anything. The clearing process depends entirely on our individual needs.

The light is switched on
Sometimes it may take a while to feel the results of an attunement. One student sent me this email the day after the course:

> *So I'm on the tube last night going home feeling very overwhelmed by the amount of knowledge received over the weekend; I connect to the underground WiFi and listen to some randomly selected music on Spotify. On comes on a song which makes me jump initially. It's by a beautiful vocalist, Delta Goodrem, and it's a song written by Prince called 'Love, Thy Will Be Done'.*

> *As I listen to the lyrics, the side of my face that has been hot all afternoon cools down and [the heat] goes into my palms as she sings about no longer resisting the guiding light and feeling peace inside.*

> *I go home and book the Reiki 2 course.*

I think this really sums up what an attunement is all about!

The Reiki lineage

An attunement adds one more unique feature to Reiki: it gives every student a *Reiki lineage*. Similar to a family tree, this grows bigger with every generation of Reiki Masters, but the trunk remains the same: Mikao Usui.

Put simply, a lineage means: I was attuned by Mr A., who was attuned by Ms B., who was attuned by Ms C. and so on, until someone was attuned by Mikao Usui. There must be an unbroken lineage going all the way back to him. If not, it is an entirely different system. Today, the lineage that involves Hawayo Takata (*see pages 206-9*) is often called the 'Western lineage' as it went through some changes after it left Japan. The lineages that exclusively stayed in Japan until recently are called 'Japanese or Eastern lineages'. A few Reiki teachers trained in both, and therefore have two or more lineages.

To give an example, this is my personal lineage:

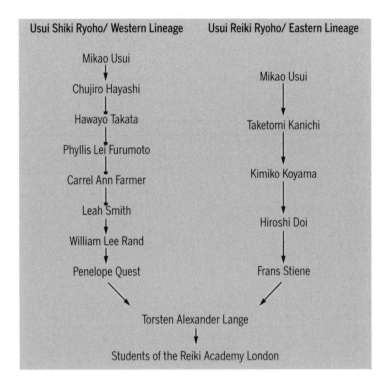

Usui Shiki Ryoho/ Western Lineage	Usui Reiki Ryoho/ Eastern Lineage
Mikao Usui	
↓	
Chujiro Hayashi	Mikao Usui
↓	↓
Hawayo Takata	Taketomi Kanichi
↓	↓
Phyllis Lei Furumoto	
↓	Kimiko Koyama
Carrel Ann Farmer	↓
↓	
Leah Smith	Hiroshi Doi
↓	↓
William Lee Rand	
↓	Frans Stiene
Penelope Quest	

Torsten Alexander Lange
↓
Students of the Reiki Academy London

Your Reiki lineage is the only way to identify if you have learned traditional Reiki – and is therefore required as proof if you want to join a Reiki association.

SUMMARY

❖ An attunement recreates Mikao Usui's moment of enlightenment.

❖ It brings the student 'in tune' with Reiki and opens up their individual connection to it.

- ❖ Everyone who has been attuned takes their place in an unbroken lineage going back to Mikao Usui.

Chapter 6

Shoden/Reiki 1:
Adjusting to the light

Once attuned, we can explore the many practical applications that bring Reiki into our everyday life.

Palm healing

Healing hands

It is probably an obvious statement, but Reiki starts with the hands. Either we receive a treatment for the first time and, much to our surprise, notice a strong sensation of heat when the practitioner's hands are placed on our body, or we receive an attunement on a Reiki course and are even more surprised: 'I can *feel* something in my hands!'

We then start experimenting with our hands. At some stage when we're giving Reiki, we may even take them off the recipient's body and place them a few centimetres away. And the connection can still be felt, the recipient can still get Reiki: the miracle is complete. When we finally get feedback, it's impossible to contain ourselves. I've had many courses where the students fell into each other's arms after giving their first Reiki treatment!

No wonder that the Western lineage of Reiki teaching focuses almost entirely on the hands. Although this has been blown slightly out of proportion, as we will see in a moment when we look at the other elements of Reiki, better too much than too little. After all, we suddenly have *healing hands*!

When we start with Reiki, it may even seem as if our hands are developing a life of their own. Not to worry – they aren't. They're nothing but a tool. They function as an extension of our inner connection to the source of Reiki – that's all!

Look at your hands

But let's start by looking at our hands – in the most literal sense. Well manicured? Clean? Soft and pretty? Or showing the signs of hard work? Any cuts or bruises, any swelling? Any deformations?

For Reiki, the outer appearance of the hands doesn't matter. However they look, they're just fine as they are. Because we don't actually use them – we let them be used.

We might not be familiar with this idea, but we all tend to be quite familiar with our hands. Consciously and subconsciously, we use them most of our waking life. They hold, make, write, type, point... We play nervously with them... Hands are pretty multifunctional.

And they can do even more: they can *touch*. They can *feel*. They can *connect*.

Have you ever walked around holding hands with someone – looking silly but not caring? Or sat in front of the TV with someone and reached out for their hand? Didn't it feel wonderful? And safe? Are you going through this phase now? Or have you never stopped? Holding hands is a sign of love. And it's the same in Reiki.

Holding something with our hands is also a sign of exploration. When we show a toy to a baby, they will immediately try to grab it. They want to hold it – even if the 'toy' is actually our spectacles. They are using their hands to find out more. This is also the same in Reiki.

When someone slips and falls on the pavement in front of you, do you wonder whether it's appropriate to offer your hand to a stranger or do you automatically stretch out your hand to help them up? Reaching out with our hands is a sign of compassion and connection. And again, it's the same in Reiki.

We have all even used our hands for healing, whether stemming blood, applying a plaster or bandage, or just giving comfort. When we see someone crying, injured or suffering in any other way, it is just natural to offer a helping hand.

And yet with Reiki something is added that wasn't there before. With Reiki we use our hands in three very novel ways:

1. To *connect* – not just physically, but energetically too.

2. To *sense* – not just bodily functions, but emotions and energy blockages.

3. To *share* – our connection to the source of Reiki.

Of course palm healing wasn't invented for the system of Reiki. As mentioned earlier, it had been used for a very long time – probably since the dawn of humankind. Healers in all cultures used their hands, and Jesus certainly with the utmost success! The only difference is that with Reiki, healing can be done by *anyone* who has been attuned. As I said before, with Reiki, healing hands got democratized. All we need to do now is to use them.

How to connect to Reiki

So, you've been on a Reiki course. And you've got healing hands. Wow! You probably still can't quite believe it works. It did on the course – but what about at home?

The first thing you have to remember is how to connect to Reiki again. Nothing is easier: just *think of* Reiki! As soon as you intend to connect, it's there in an instant. I tend to state silently to myself (and to the universe of course): 'I intend to connect to Reiki.' Some people prefer to 'ask for' Reiki – or ask Reiki 'for help'. Anything works, as long as the intention is there. Either consciously or subconsciously.

Occasionally, you may even be sitting watching TV and suddenly find your palms getting warm. Once you are attuned, Reiki comes when needed, not just when asked. It simply switches itself on.

Do you need to do anything with your hands when you connect? Although, again, there is no set rule, many practitioners like to place their hands in a particular position. I tend just to open my hands with the palms facing up. Others stretch up their arms and raise their hands above their head. Or you can place your hands in *Gassho*, the prayer position (*see page 126*). All these gestures can help you to focus on your hands as tools for Reiki and imply that you are about to receive something special.

Now just wait for a moment until you can feel the connection – either physically as a sensation in your palms or as an inner awareness – and you're ready to start.

Start with yourself

You can now place your healing hands on anything and everything, anyone and everyone. As you surely will. But first things first: don't forget yourself!

Even if your primary goal is to practise Reiki as an alternative therapy, or you've learned it to treat a loved one who is ill, the starting-point is always your *own* inner connection to it. The more you use it for yourself, the stronger that connection will become. In a moment, we will look at using practices like meditation and breathing to deepen this connection. But the simplest way is to use your healing hands!

If you can place your hands on others for healing, it naturally follows that you can also place them on yourself. In the Western tradition, this is called a *self-treatment*. I start every day with it.

It works in a variety of ways:

❖ It brings a degree of harmony and balance.

❖ It works on our physical health.

❖ It clears energy blockages.

- We feel more energetic and focused during the day.

- We may receive intuitive ideas for the day.

- We become more aligned with the universe.

- And it feels great. I often think it's like getting a hug from God!

It works best when we create a daily routine. Personally, my preferred time for self-treatment is in the morning, before I get up. If I don't do it first thing, I find it hard to make the time later in the day. But you may be more organized and prefer to go for the time when the kids have left for school, or your lunch break, or the evening, just before you go to bed. Any time is fine. What is key is the regularity.

For my morning treatments, I use a little trick: I set the alarm for 30 minutes before I'm due to get up. Then, as soon as it rings, I reset it for half an hour later, creating a short period when I don't need to worry about time-keeping and can concentrate fully on Reiki, knowing that if I nod off during the treatment, I'll still be able to get up in time for work. Admittedly, I *have* fallen asleep again on the odd occasion, but even then the Reiki works (*see also the case study on page 90*). Also, I tend to find that I somehow get this half-hour back during the day. The day runs more smoothly and I am more energetic.

My step-by-step guide to self-treatment is below. However, there's no need to follow it rigidly. You'll soon find that your intuition will lead the way. The following set of hand positions, although used by most Reiki practitioners, is only a suggestion.

Before you start, be prepared for the unexpected. Just a few days into my own Reiki practice something *rather* unexpected happened. I'm glad I'd read about it beforehand (although of course I didn't believe it would happen to me). Quite simply, my hands took over! I'd just spent a few minutes with them on my heart chakra and wanted to move them to the next position – and they didn't follow. They were stuck! Or at least it felt that way. Obviously I was meant to stay with the heart for a bit longer, which I duly did. Needless to say, it wasn't really the hands taking over – it was just Reiki leading the way.

Today I sometimes use the entire set of hand positions, other times just two or three positions. There's nothing better than intuition overriding rules! But the classic hand positions of the Western tradition are a great starting-point:

Exercise: How to give a self-treatment

❖ Connect to Reiki, wait until you feel a sensation in your hands or you just feel you're ready and then place your hands in the first position...

❖ Hold each position for three to five minutes. Initially, you may find it tedious to hold a position for such a long time, but after a few treatments your 'Reiki muscles' will have strengthened and you'll have no further problems with it. (If you have any particular physical problems, simply place your hands straight on these areas.)

1. *Top of the head:* Place one of your hands on the back of your head and the other on your crown. (Alternatively, you can place both your hands on or near your crown.)

2. *Eyes:* Cup your hands over your eyes (your wrists may rest on your cheekbones, your fingertips on your forehead).

3. *Ears:* Cup your hands around your ears.

4. *Throat:* Place your hands with your thumbs on your collarbones, palms towards your throat. (Alternatively, place your hands either side of your neck.)

The classic hand positions for a self-treatment

5. *Heart chakra:* Place your hands on your upper chest at the level of your heart.

6. *Solar plexus:* Place your hands at the lower end of your ribcage.

7. *Navel chakra:* Place your hands about 2cm (1 in) below your navel.

8. *Root chakra:* Place your hands on either side of your hips or more towards the centre of your body, whichever you prefer (after all, it is your own body).

9. In addition, you may place your hands on your back or legs, wherever you feel is comfortable and required.

The classic hand positions for a self-treatment (continued)

Sharing Reiki with others

Amazingly, Reiki can be used to treat other people straight away. Don't let anything stop you! Some students go home after the first day of the course and try it out on their family. The feedback the next day is fabulous.

The term 'treating others' isn't, however, wholly appropriate. We don't really give a treatment, we merely open up to Reiki and share the connection with the client. Students often comment in surprise that after 'giving a treatment' they feel as if they've received one. And that is exactly what happens.

When we practise Reiki, we don't use any of our own energy, we simply connect to energy from above. (Which is why some practitioners use the term 'channelling energy'.) Unlike our own energy, Reiki is available in abundance. Sharing it will never leave us depleted.

In this chapter we will explore the basics of providing a Reiki treatment. They are always the same, no matter whether you're a complete novice or a seasoned practitioner.

Who can be treated?

Everyone! Friends, family, the whole world. Although officially after Reiki 1 you're supposed only to treat friends and family. But where's the boundary? Isn't everybody a friend in a way? The difference lies in money matters. As soon as you charge for a treatment (even for family and friends), you're running a business. And for that you need to have public liability insurance. But as long as you do it for free, you can treat anyone you like (unless, of course, they don't want Reiki).

At least, this is what applies in the UK. In other countries, including a number of states in the USA, where each one seems to have a different law concerning complementary therapies, you may find stricter regulation. It's best to check it out before you place your hands on anybody! Some states, for instance, require a Reiki practitioner to be a licensed sports masseur before they can give professional treatments. If in doubt, you can always play it safe: simply place your hands a few centimetres away from the body. As long as there's no touch involved, there are no concerns. And there's no difference in the effectiveness of the treatment either.

What can be treated?
Everything! Just to alleviate any doubts, I would like to repeat this: absolutely everything can be treated! There is no condition that will not benefit from Reiki. I've had students using it on people suffering with everything from back pain to cancer, bruises to dementia, alcoholism to relationship problems. One student treated the aching hands of her pianist husband straight after her Reiki 1 course. He happily resumed playing the next day.

There are also no exclusions when it comes to the conditions a recipient might have. Pregnancy, a pacemaker and medication are no reasons not to give Reiki. In the first case, you will be treating two in one; in the second, the machine will be assisted; in the last, the effects will be maximized and side effects minimized.

You can't go wrong
Reiki is not only popular because of its healing success but also because it is entirely risk-free. Used on its own,

it cannot do any harm. And that's official: the National Occupational Standards (NOS) for Reiki Practice in the UK state that 'there are no known contra-indications to Reiki when used on its own'.[1] The only side effect is spiritual development.

Still, many people find this difficult to accept. Deep in the recesses of our mind we have an ingrained fear that there might still be exceptions and that just this once something will go wrong. After a lifetime of negative conditioning, this isn't surprising: with medical treatment, we are told that every remedy has side effects and all good medicine tastes bitter. If we aren't suffering, we don't think it's working. In the moral and religious sphere, too, at least a certain degree of punishment is often expected, even from God. So how can Reiki be without any negativity at all? Well, it just *is*.

Sadly, there is a huge need to emphasize this, because people seem to be unaware of it. The internet, for example, is full of disconcerting stories and strange advice about Reiki. But all the stories start along the lines of 'I heard of someone who...' or 'I was told that this or that happened...' If you investigate more deeply, they turn out to be hearsay. Or simply assumptions.

Of course, in conventional terms it would make sense to check whether a certain therapy could have a negative effect on a client with a pacemaker, or suffering from asthma, epilepsy, diabetes or high blood pressure. For Reiki, though, this has all been tested. In fact, many practitioners have stated that they have found Reiki particularly helpful for the conditions just listed.

If there had ever been a verifiable problem with the use of Reiki, surely the NOS would not have used the above wording. And, frankly, I would have walked away from it. I practise Reiki because I trust it completely. Obviously, insurance companies do too: if the premium for public liability insurance is an indicator of risk, it seems they consider Reiki entirely risk-free. The policy for Reiki costs a fraction of those for many other therapies.

The worst thing that can happen when giving Reiki is that the recipient doesn't feel anything. If this is the case (although it's quite rare in my experience), don't get too frustrated. If other people feel something and this person does not, there must be a reason for it. Maybe they aren't ready to face change. Maybe they are consciously or subconsciously resisting the treatment. Personally, I wouldn't spend too much time worrying about it. You have offered Reiki and that is all you can do.

Getting technical

Before we get started with the actual treatment, we need to make some preparations. This is my suggested 'to do' list:

Find a place

A treatment can be given anywhere: on a bench in the park, on a towel on the beach. Basically, wherever you are. But in most cases you would look for somewhere quiet and sheltered. I tend to find that the best place for this is *home* – either yours or the client's. There's no need for a separate treatment room. When I started my practice, I simply moved the sofa and TV to the side of the room and placed the treatment couch in the middle. I never had a client who felt this was inappropriate.

If you aren't comfortable inviting potential strangers into your home, you may want to make sure that a family member is also present in the house. Or you could rent a therapy room. In many complementary therapy clinics, rooms can be hired by the hour – just shop around to get a good deal.

Prepare the space

Now you need a place for the client to lie down comfortably. This can be on an armchair, sofa, bed, sturdy dining table or even yoga mat on the floor. Some clients might prefer to sit. That's also fine. Just make sure that *you* are comfortable, too. You may have the best of intentions, but leaning over in an awkward position or kneeling down on a hard floor isn't ideal. By the end of the treatment you will find yourself in need of Reiki too. So make sure that you have something to sit on (maybe a cushion on the floor) and check your posture. If you happen to find that you are uncomfortable at any time during the treatment, you can always lift your hands for a moment, adjust your position and then put them back again.

If you give treatments regularly, you may want to consider investing in a treatment couch. Most of them fold away and are light enough to carry. There are many surprisingly cheap offers available. Any therapy couch will be fine, but if you go for a dedicated Reiki couch you will have the benefit of no crossing bar at the head and foot end, which allows you to sit slightly closer to the client. Some even come with a stool.

It is good practice to cover the client with a blanket, as often the body temperature drops when we relax. I even cover clients in summer (just using a simple sheet), as I don't want the sensation of Reiki energy being confused with body heat and touch on naked skin.

Your home (or wherever else you are giving the treatment) now transforms into a healing space and you may want to spend a moment preparing it appropriately. This doesn't mean you have to redecorate or move half of your furniture! Some tidying and airing will be perfectly fine. Some practitioners also light a candle or an incense stick or burn essential oils. Just be careful not to overdo it, as some clients' senses heighten during the treatment. You don't want them to start coughing because of your lavender oil.

Finally, make sure to switch off all phones and any other noise-making devices you may use. Although not a disaster, it tends to be a bit disconcerting when a phone rings in the middle of a treatment.

Prepare yourself
It's a good idea not to chew on a raw garlic bulb just before the treatment. However healthy this may be, leave it for afterwards. Pouring a bottle of perfume over yourself is also a bit much. Just washing your hands will be perfectly fine.

What you wear is entirely up to you – there's no need for any special clothing. The practical aspects are more important: you want your clothes to be comfortable. Also, you may get warm or cold after a while, so dress in layers and have a cardigan handy.

It's also a good idea to take off any chunky pieces of jewellery. You don't want them dangling in your client's face.

Finally, do you need to protect yourself during a Reiki treatment? The answer is a clear *no*. I am aware that this is contrary to what is often published, but I have never used any kind of protection before giving a treatment. I've never even thought about it! Reiki is pure light – there's no room for any shadows. We're not inviting any negative energy in during a treatment – all we're doing is releasing it. We may notice fear and trauma coming to the surface – but we can rest assured that Reiki will deal with it.

Prepare the client

A first-time client is often rather nervous. They don't know what to expect and may have had unpleasant experiences with other therapies. But even if they've had Reiki before, it's still good to remind them of the basics:

❖ The client stays completely clothed throughout the treatment (but of course can take off heavy items of clothing and shoes).

❖ Chunky jewellery should be taken off (we don't want the client to strangle themselves), as well as spectacles, watches and hearing aids. If they prefer to keep any of these on, it won't be a problem, though – just adjust your hand positions to avoid touching these items.

❖ Ask the client if they have any particular issues or areas they would like to be treated.

❖ Let them know what they may experience: localized hot or cold sensations; signs of release, such as sudden body movements, coughing or feeling emotional; flashbacks, images or film-like scenes. They may also experience very little and the results may not be immediate.

❖ Reassure them that there's nothing to worry about. Reiki is entirely safe and they should just relax and close their eyes.

❖ Also ask them to let you know if they want you to move or lift your hands at any time – and don't panic if they actually do! It will only happen very rarely and is just a sign that they are feeling something quite intensely.

On or off
Finally, make sure to ask before the treatment whether the client would like you to place your hands on their body or keep them slightly away.

With regards to physical touch, the following considerations apply:

❖ Hands-on or -off treatments are equally valid and effective (you should give and receive at least one hands-off treatment yourself to see how it feels).

❖ The majority of people will be fine with a hands-on treatment.

❖ If someone prefers your hands to be kept away, don't make this an issue! There may be a variety of reasons for it: they've had a traumatic experience in the past; they feel it's too personal; they simply don't like it; they've just been to the hairdresser's and don't want the result messed up. In every case, they'll be embarrassed to tell you, and there's no need to ask.

- ❖ Never place your hands where it might be deemed inappropriate. There is absolutely no need ever to place them on any private areas. You can always hold them slightly above these areas or place them on the sides of the body or an adequate distance from the area in need of Reiki.

- ❖ When you place your hands on the body, be neither too light with your touch nor apply pressure (Reiki is not a massage). When the hands barely touch, they tend to shake and the client will feel insecure. If you apply pressure, you are manipulating the body, and this isn't accepted as part of a contemporary Reiki treatment. Simply rest your hands on the body, just as you would on the delicate arm of a sofa.

How often, how long?

You cannot overdo Reiki, but you can underdo it. As it is impossible to do any damage with it, in theory a treatment can be given for as long as you like. The recipient will automatically stop to 'draw' the energy when they've had enough for the moment. In most cases, however, it isn't necessary to give a treatment for longer than 30 minutes (for a specific area of the body) or 45 to 60 minutes (for a full treatment) at a time. (If you are treating a very serious condition, it's not a problem to give Reiki for longer, or several times during the day.) As Reiki stimulates the body's innate self-healing abilities, the body also needs some time to rest and heal after treatment. After a few treatments, you'll intuitively know when you can stop the treatment.

A single treatment can work wonders and result in physical healing or a change in perception. This happens surprisingly often in fact. You and the recipient may then happily leave it at this one appointment. But in other cases, more treatments are needed – maybe two or three, maybe 30 or 100. Don't give up if the first treatment doesn't bring complete healing. When Hawayo Takata (*see page 18*) gave treatments for severe or chronic illnesses, after a few weeks she often offered to teach a family member Reiki so that they could carry on giving treatments for the next month or two. Healing can take time. Most illnesses don't appear overnight. Undoing them can be a lengthy process too. So, if the result you're hoping for doesn't manifest immediately, just carry on. Reiki should only be stopped when the symptoms are gone or you have other results that are sufficient.

I've occasionally found that even a few minutes of Reiki can do the job. Miracles don't have a time-frame. But generally I would say that a five or 10-minute treatment isn't really a treatment, it's a taster – or an emergency treatment. It's great to start with, but hopefully the recipient will come back for more. Even in our fast-paced lives, we should give Reiki the time and respect it is due.

The perfect Reiki treatment

...is one that doesn't go to plan. But don't worry – you can leave everything to Reiki. It's perfectly safe. Let intuition take over and just accept that whatever this treatment brings is whatever is right for the client at this moment.

And yet, for all this, giving your first Reiki treatment can be a bit nerve-wracking. You look at this person in front of you and suddenly think: *What have I got myself into? This person is here to get a Reiki treatment – from me!*

I was very nervous when I gave my first Reiki treatment. Would I do everything correctly? Would the person feel anything? You might feel the same, but again, don't worry. Reiki is *doing without doing*.[2] It isn't about *you*, it's about *Reiki*. The more we simply accept this, the more open we will be, and the more Reiki will be felt.

Reiki practitioner Pamela Miles writes: '...as I have practised over two decades, it's become obvious to me that the less I do and the quieter I am inside, the more room there is for Reiki.'[3]

Giving a Reiki treatment ultimately boils down to two simple steps:

1. Connect to Reiki.
2. Place your hands wherever they are needed.

The first we do by intention, the second by intuition. That's all.

Having said this, though, it's both possible and helpful to elaborate on these basic steps. If somebody bruises their shoulder, we connect to Reiki and of course place our hand straight on the shoulder. As we would in an emergency. But for a normal Reiki treatment, most people would add a few more steps. This is the classic sequence:

1. Prepare for Reiki.
2. Set your intention.
3. Connect to Reiki.
4. Feel the connection.
5. Connect with the client.
6. Place the hands.
7. Follow your intuition.
8. Send Reiki into the aura.
9. Smooth down the aura.
10. Conclude the treatment.
11. Thank Reiki.
12. Ground yourself.

As most likely this will be the basis for giving Reiki treatments for the rest of your life, I will now go into it in much more detail. A step-by-step example of how I give a treatment is shown on the following pages. But again, it's not a rigid structure. Please take it as a guideline – and develop your own routine.

What to think of during the treatment

Before we start, one last little piece of advice. This question often pops up on my courses: 'Do you need to think of something specific?' No – and yes. If, as soon as you start the treatment, you mentally create a 'to do' list for the week or start thinking of your tax return, you'll be too distracted. Most likely neither you nor your client will feel much Reiki. Needless to say, you wouldn't do this anyway...

The best way to approach the treatment is to focus on your hands. Do you feel a sensation? Does it change after a while? Do you get any ideas about the condition or the person you are treating?

And don't try too hard. I often just sit and enjoy the wonderful sensation of feeling connected. Soon you will enter a meditative state. A few of my students call it 'Reiki Land'.

After a few treatments, you won't worry about this anyway. Reiki will just take you to where you need to be. Yet it's not always easy to stay alert for an entire hour. Occasionally you may find your mind wandering off. Don't worry if you're distracted for a moment. Once you do notice it, gently bring yourself back to Reiki and carry on. Reiki will have carried on.

My student Dee provided a brilliant example of this. She gave Reiki to her husband, who had dislocated his shoulder in a motorbike accident. It was so painful that he could only bear it being touched when his wife used Reiki. One evening, lying in bed, she reached over to place her hand on his shoulder and give him some more Reiki. Then she nodded off. A few minutes later, he started to call out: 'Wake up, wake up! It's getting too warm!' Even though the practitioner was asleep, Reiki had just carried on working...

From experiences like this, I conclude that *intention* is a major factor in using Reiki. It almost seems that we enter into an agreement with the universe when we decide to use it.

So, finally, let's start the treatment.

Exercise: The perfect Reiki treatment

The client is now comfortably placed on whatever is available: sofa, bed, yoga mat, sturdy dining table or professional treatment couch. (Please be sure to place a cushion under their knees to alleviate any strain from the lower back.) Ask them to close their eyes so that they can relax. Then get ready yourself:

1. Prepare for Reiki
I start with dry bathing (*Kenyoku-Ho, see page 131*) or a Reiki shower (*page 133*) to remove any mental or physical energy blockages and then take a moment to calm down and relax. Take as much time as you need. Your client is happily lying down and won't mind waiting another minute or two.

2. Set your intention

Do this in whichever way is best for you. I place my hands in *Gassho* (*see page 126*) for a moment to centre myself, then set my intention to give a Reiki treatment.

3. Connect to Reiki

I just state to myself (and to the universe): 'I intend to connect to Reiki.'

4. Feel the connection

Wait until you *feel* the Reiki energy. This is very important. Take your time. You might feel a sensation in your palms or simply have the awareness that you are now connected. (Deep abdominal breathing [*see page 129*] can help here.)

5. Connect with the client

Standing beside the client, I slowly lower my hands, intending to make a connection with the client's aura/energy body. I spend a moment sensing this. (If this step causes any difficulties, just leave it out. It is by no means essential.)

6. Place the hands

After this, I finally place my hands on the body (or slightly away from it, whichever has been agreed and is appropriate). There are several options:

❖ Using the classic sequence of 12 hand positions as taught by Hawayo Takata and used by the majority of Reiki practitioners (*see pages 93–95*). Hold each position for three to five minutes or as long as feels right.

❖ Going straight to the problem area (if this is clearly identifiable).

❖ Using the body-scanning or *Reiji-Ho* method (*see page 169*) to determine where to place the hands.

❖ Any combination of the above. (Please note that it feels more comfortable for the client if only one hand is moved at a time.)

7. Follow your intuition
Even if you are following a set sequence of hand positions or the client has asked you to place your hands on a particular area, still listen to your intuition. It's perfectly fine to end up using only one or two hand positions for the entire treatment. In fact, I tend to find that a very quick succession of positions indicates that the practitioner is rather inexperienced and hasn't learned to trust their intuition yet.

8. Send Reiki into the aura
Before I finish I spend a moment sending Reiki into the client's aura. I don't think many practitioners do this, but I like to sense the connection with the entire 'energy person' at the end of the treatment. I slowly raise my hands with the intention of bringing Reiki into all the layers of the aura.

9. Smooth down the aura
At the end of a treatment most practitioners 'smooth down' the aura. To do this, the hands are moved over the body from the head to the feet (a bit like stroking a pet, only with the hands a few centimetres away from the body). This is normally done three times. The idea behind it is that stale energy may have been released during the treatment and needs to be cleared out of the body. But don't worry if you forget to do this – I'm sure the stale energy will disappear of its own accord. After all, you've just given Reiki!

10. Conclude the treatment
You now need to make the client aware that the treatment is over and bring them back from their wonderfully serene and peaceful state. Or, if they are asleep, wake them up. In either case, you need to be gentle (a bucket of cold water is not ideal). I normally place my hand on

their shoulder and tell them in a low voice that the treatment is now complete and they may take as much time as they need to come back to the here and now. Or I use the backstroke, applying gentle pressure with the knuckles of my index and middle fingers on either side of the spine (not in the middle!) and making three swift movements towards the lower back. This technique is used in many hands-on therapies.

11. Thank Reiki

I then place my hands in *Gassho* for a moment and thank Reiki. After all, it wasn't me who gave the treatment – I was just lending my hands.

12. Ground yourself

Dry brushing concludes the treatment. This grounds me and brings me back to the here and now.

You should offer the client a glass of water after the treatment (to help flush out any toxins released from the body) and advise them to drink plenty of water for the rest of the day (for the same reason).

The classic (Western-style) hand positions for giving a treatment to others:

1. Top of the head: Standing or sitting at the head end of the treatment couch, place one of your hands underneath the client's head and the other on the crown. (Alternatively, or if you are giving a hands-off treatment, place both hands on or near the crown.)

2. Eyes: Cup your hands over the eyes (your wrists may rest on the client's forehead).

3. *Ears:* Cup your hands around the ears.

4. *Throat:* Place your hands with the little fingers on the collarbones, palms towards the throat. (Alternatively, place your hands either side of the neck.)

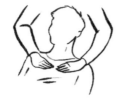

5. *Heart chakra:* If you can lean forward further, place your hands on the upper chest of the client. Otherwise, stand beside the client.

6. *Solar plexus:* Stand beside the client and place your hands at the lower end of the ribcage.

7. *Navel chakra:* Place your hands about 2cm (1 in) below the navel, roughly where a belt would be worn.

8. *Root chakra:* Place your hands on either side of the hips.

Now you have a choice: in the Western tradition, the client is asked to turn over and lie on their front. But if this is difficult, or they don't want to, you may carry on with the treatment with the client lying on their back. (In this case, the next positions are the thighs, the knees, the shins and the feet.) If the client does turn over, please move the cushion to the ankles and position your hands as follows:

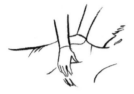

9. *Shoulder blades:* Place one hand on each shoulder blade.

10. *Middle back:* Place both hands halfway between the shoulder blades and the waist.

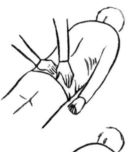

11. *Waist:* Place your hands on the back at waist level.

12. *Buttocks:* Place your hands on or above the buttocks.

'What have I done?'

And that may be exactly what you say next! Did it work? What really happened?

Wait for your client to come back into the here and now and then start to make some sense of their experiences. Although both of you, practitioner and client, will have had experiences, I tend to ask the client first what they want to share.

The more treatments you give, the more you'll start to see some patterns in the effects they have. And yet no two Reiki treatments are exactly the same. Every treatment teaches us something new. Here is my personal – and by no means exhaustive – list of the effects you may encounter both during and after a treatment. They are meant for reference – and to help you make a bit more sense of the experiences you will have.

Experiences and effects during a treatment

Sleep

Probably the most unexciting result! But Reiki tends to have a relaxing effect and clients fall asleep quite frequently. (The first ones to do so are normally those who complain that they have sleeping problems.) As sleep is a natural healing state for the body, I usually leave them to snore away happily. If the snoring does get too much, you can always gently place your hand on their shoulder and ask them to move, maybe to lie on their side or front so that falling asleep again will be a bit more difficult. I am certain, though, that a Reiki treatment is just as effective when the client dozes off...

Drifting off
Even clients who don't fall asleep often comment that they were 'drifting off' during the treatment. If they are used to meditating, they may describe this as a familiar meditative state; if they are new to it, they tend to talk about 'a happy place' or 'a peaceful place' or 'a floating sensation'. It is the start of leaving the restrictions of our physical existence behind and experiencing our spiritual being.

Localized physical sensations
Most recipients feel a strong sensation of _heat_ in the area where the practitioner's hands are placed. Some even feel this as uncomfortably strong. (It can be eased by slightly lifting the hands.) Others experience the opposite: a localized sensation of _cold_. Both mean the same: Reiki is at work. Other signs of this may be tingling, slight numbness and heaviness. Occasionally, even a localized sensation of pain can occur. None of this is anything to worry about; it all shows that something is shifting in the body.

Release...
...comes in different shapes and sizes: _sudden body movements_, _coughing_ and _crying_ are all signs that physical or emotional tension is being released. So don't worry if your client suddenly starts sobbing. Just offer them a tissue and ask them to take their time in composing themselves. You can then either continue the treatment or decide that the objective has been achieved (no, not making them cry, but bringing something out that stirred those emotions) and leave it for the day. Just ask them what they prefer.

Some clients may even start to laugh. That's a great way to feel better – simply join in!

Ideas
It can happen that a client arrives bothered by a non-physical problem – and suddenly comes up with a smart solution.

Colours and shapes
Many people see colours and shapes, often resembling slow-moving works of abstract art. Of course, colours and shapes are ways of perceiving the movement of energy *visually*.

Signs and symbols
Some people see a particular image – a tree, an animal, a house, a car or a star, to name but a few. Some even see abstract symbols similar to the ones introduced in Reiki 2.

One of my Reiki 1 students saw the image of a pansy appearing during the first Reiki treatment she received from a fellow student on the course. Strangely, the pansy didn't have any dark inner areas and was completely golden in colour. After some soul-searching, the student decided it must be a sign that she should spend more time in nature, echoing an urge she had already had for a while. Running a bit late the next morning, she missed her train and had to wait half an hour for the next one. When she finally got on it and sat down, she looked out of the window and saw a large lorry approaching. On it was a big logo: a golden pansy (without the usual black inside) on a green background. Next to it was a slogan: 'Closer to nature.' What a fabulous example of synchronicity!

Moving images

Occasionally clients see an entire story unfolding in front of their closed eyes, just as if they were watching a movie. This can have a dream-like quality and often makes sense only days or weeks after the treatment, when it either takes place in reality or they suddenly get an idea of its meaning.

Memories

When memories come up (often as if they are being relived rather than remembered), they are usually not of recent experiences but long-forgotten ones. This means the person is now ready to deal with them.

Feeling a presence

It's not unusual for clients to feel a non-physical presence during the treatment. This may be a guide or angel, or a friend or family member saying hello from the spirit realm. I've had several clients mention having complete conversations with their mother or father who had been 'dead' for many years.

Having an out-of-body experience

Some even feel they are leaving their body. They feel weightless and unrestricted by the physical limitations of their body.

Little or nothing

And if *little or nothing* of the above happens and the client simply reports a feeling of relaxation, that's perfectly fine. The other experiences are only listed because they *may* happen – and I don't want you to freak out if they do. They are perfectly normal – but not necessary. Healing will take place even if neither the client nor the practitioner feels very much at all. Just wait for the feedback a while later!

Experiences and effects straight after a treatment

Pain is better
In many cases, clients find that the physical problem they are suffering from has improved. Sometimes dramatically.

Pain is worse
In other cases, the opposite happens. Although initially perplexing, this so-called 'healing crisis' is a well-known effect in many therapies, not just in Reiki. It means that something is shifting and the physical healing process has started, although the initial efforts are causing pain. It's similar to the sensation when we cut ourselves: we look at the bleeding wound and don't feel anything at all. We put it under cold water, apply a plaster – and suddenly the pain kicks in. This is when the actual healing starts.

A healing crisis can last between an hour and a day, but not longer. Experienced Reiki practitioners just smile when somebody complains about feeling a bit worse after the treatment and reassure them that they will feel the opposite soon.

Not much has changed
In many cases, the immediate effect is only subtle – barely noticeable – as the body needs some time before the big change happens. Often the main improvement takes

place over the following day or two. The long-lost virtue of patience comes in handy here.

An idea about the cause
It can also happen that a client comes out of a treatment with a clear idea of what they can do to resolve a problem (physical or otherwise) and/or what (often seemingly unrelated) caused it in the first place.

Not quite back
Some clients look slightly dazed after the treatment. They mumble words like 'weird', 'strange' or 'odd' and need some time to digest what's happened to them. I suggest they drink plenty of water, have some fresh air and spend some time on their own. Encouraging them to do dry brushing (*see page 131*) will also help them to come back to the here and now more quickly.

Something has come to the surface
In a similar way to a physical healing crisis, it may happen that a client feels emotionally unwell. Some feel sad, some even angry – not about the treatment but about a memory that has surfaced. This will be something they now have to deal with. But the fact that it has come out means they are able to do this – and of course they have the support of Reiki.

Smiling all over
And again, the opposite may happen: sometimes a client just oozes happiness, relief and wellbeing.

Long-term effects

Whatever a person is suffering from, Reiki can have a huge impact on:

Taking action

Either consciously or subconsciously, the Reiki client may implement changes to their lifestyle.

Gaining more strength

People often have noticeably more strength to deal with life.

Acquiring new perception

People see things in a different light, change their attitude, have more understanding and can accept and forgive others.

Releasing toxins

A Reiki treatment starts a cleansing process in the body in a similar way to an attunement (*see page 65*).

Changing circumstances

Miraculous changes can happen around a person who has had a Reiki treatment. Synchronicity arrives...

Expect the unexpected

Sometimes Reiki sets a whole chain of events in motion. A practitioner friend of mine, for instance, gave a treatment to a man in his thirties. Although his strong physique and positive attitude would not normally have suggested this, he suffered from regular panic attacks with severe breathing problems. He received a full Reiki treatment, and his girlfriend, who had accompanied him, had a shorter one. The practitioner noted a lot of Reiki being drawn into the man's chest and held her hands there for longer than in other positions.

Driving home, the man suddenly suffered another panic attack. Luckily his girlfriend was able to take over and drive him straight to the nearest hospital. She knew how relaxed they both felt after the Reiki treatment – this couldn't be a panic attack!

As usual, though, at A&E the man was diagnosed with a panic attack. He was about to be sent home when his girlfriend stepped in, told the doctors about the Reiki treatment and that she didn't believe that a panic attack could happen straight afterwards, and insisted on a proper check-up. A blood test then revealed a potential problem: the man was so dehydrated that it was difficult to extract any blood at all. Finally alerted to the fact that there was a serious issue here, the doctors ordered an MRI scan and discovered three blood clots in the lungs.

Half an hour later my friend received a text message from the girlfriend: 'You saved his life!' The man could now receive the correct treatment. Two months later he went back to work.

Even if Reiki doesn't seem to work, we may discover a hidden reason why. I once used it for a slipped disc in my back. Thirty minutes later the pain had almost gone and the neck had somehow readjusted itself. When I tried to do the same with my painful right shoulder, it didn't work.

Reluctantly I saw my GP, who prescribed physiotherapy. Being shown how to correct my posture and given some simple exercises really helped me and the pain disappeared. Had I not seen the therapist, I would have carried on sitting in the wrong position and given myself the same problem again and again.

Experiences of the practitioner

When you give a treatment, you're working within the client's energy field. It is therefore highly probable that you'll have the same experiences they do. Sometimes you may even feel their problems in your own body, for example a pain in your left leg or your chest. This is nothing to worry about: you won't take on their problems, simply experience them for a brief moment. Experiences like this are a way for you to draw on your intuition and use it to shed some light on their condition.

On very rare occasions you may also come across another phenomenon: you may need Reiki more than your client! A few times on my courses the recipient has had an insight – about the *practitioner*.

Interpreting results

Unsurprisingly, many clients are slightly confused after the first treatment. Amazed, but puzzled. They will need some time to come to terms with the experience. Some choose to spend some time by themselves – and may leave rather abruptly. Don't take this personally, it's just a coping mechanism. Even if your client does stay around for a while, it's good to recommend spending a few moments outside in the fresh air. Other clients, however, feel the urge to talk.

Faced with an array of unusual experiences, they may ask you for explanations.

Here are a few words of advice on this:

❖ *Don't try too hard.*

'Why did I see red?' a client might ask. 'What does the image of a tree in bloom mean?'

I tend to ask back: 'What do *you* think it means?'

Often the client will then intuitively come up with an explanation. If not, use your own intuition. Don't make something up, though – if you don't have a firm idea, just ask the client to be patient. I tend to find that an explanation arrives a while later. Occasionally, though, the client just has to accept that whatever they saw was an experience – and leave it as such.

❖ *Don't make it too long.*

Many people can easily spend an hour or more discussing their experiences. But that isn't the point. The experiences were there to be *experienced*. Afterwards, the client should allow themselves some time simply to digest them.

❖ *Don't diagnose.*

The one thing a Reiki practitioner is not allowed to do is to diagnose an illness. If you suspect that a problem is of a physical nature, simply say that you felt a lot of Reiki being drawn into a particular area and suggest that the client has this checked out by a doctor.

- *Don't expect that the results will be exactly as you imagined.*

  They may – but they may be completely different. As I explained earlier, a cure isn't *always* what we get. In many cases it is, so please don't be disheartened if it doesn't happen immediately. Reiki *is* very much about physical healing. Only it doesn't stop there. Healing isn't always curing. So, if you don't get the results you hoped for, try to accept this and understand what is happening.

When we give a Reiki treatment, we do it for a purpose. Whether it's for ourselves or for others, we hope for an effect, we hope for healing – basically, we hope for an improvement in our current situation. We hope for physical, emotional and circumstantial change. And, as I never tire of repeating, Reiki does tend to bring this. But healing can come in an unexpected package and there may be something of a process involved.

When not to give Reiki

So that's the perfect Reiki treatment. And you can give it to anyone – can't you?

Of course you can. As I mentioned earlier, the only reason not to give Reiki is that someone doesn't want to receive it.

If a client has a heavy cold or any other contagious illness, however, you should take the normal precautions not to catch it yourself.

Also, there are situations in which Reiki must only be given *in addition* to other treatments:

- *Accidents:* Reiki can be given in addition to classic first aid, but (of course) an ambulance needs to be called.

- *Red flag symptoms:* If someone has a condition requiring immediate medical attention, Reiki must not be given in place of consulting a healthcare professional.

But this is all common sense – and hypothetical, as normally in these cases a person would see a GP or emergency doctor anyway.

Alternative or complementary?

Reiki is an alternative as well as a complementary therapy. The decision about how to use it can only be made by the client.

Many people use it as a complementary therapy – in other words, complementing traditional therapies. This is perfectly safe. Reiki can be given before, during or after surgery and alongside any medication. It can even be given to the *medication* in order to minimize side effects and maximize results. Often clients need smaller dosages as a result.

If people don't want conventional treatment, they may seek Reiki as the sole therapy. A friend once asked a Reiki practitioner to send Reiki while she had dental work done – and managed to get through the process without anaesthetic. If a client wishes to have Reiki instead of a major conventional treatment, however, the practitioner should get written confirmation from them (*see page 187*).

Of course, Reiki can also be combined with other alternative therapies. Personally, I would always use it on its own first. If you then feel drawn to combining it with other modalities, this is up to you. But I tend to find that once it's been tried, there's often no need for anything else.

Not just the hands

A Reiki treatment can also be given without the hands. Although in practice the following techniques are rarely used, they may come in handy (sorry!) when using your hands isn't appropriate or possible.

Exercise: *Gyoshi-Ho:* Sending Reiki with the eyes

❖ Connect to Reiki.

❖ If you have taken Reiki 2, you may want to draw the Power Symbol with your eyes. If not, just leave this step out.

❖ Gaze with soft, unfocused eyes at the part of the body or the person/object to whom/which you are sending Reiki.

❖ Feel or visualize Reiki being sent with your eyes.

❖ Continue until you sense that the other person/the object has now drawn in enough Reiki.

Exercise: *Koki-Ho:* Sending Reiki with the breath

❖ Connect to Reiki.

❖ Take a deep breath in, then bring your lips together.

❖ If you have taken Reiki 2, draw the Power Symbol with your tongue (if not, just leave this step out), then keep the tongue pressed against your upper teeth. If not, just leave this step out.

❖ Opening your lips only slightly, breathe out forcefully at the area in need from a distance of 10–20cm (4–8 in). Continue for 5–10 minutes, breathing in through your nose and out through your slightly closed mouth.

Exercise: Giving Reiki with the feet

Apart from the seven main chakras, we also have chakras in our palms and on the soles of our feet. Students frequently feel their feet getting hot during an attunement – a sign that these energy centres are being activated.

Mikao Usui is said to have used his feet in addition to his hands when he treated the injured after the Kanto Earthquake.

There are no traditional rules for using your feet for a Reiki treatment – just follow your intuition (but of course don't actually *stand* on the other person).

Exercise: Giving Reiki with the aura

For this technique you share Reiki with others through your aura.

❖ Start by filling your aura with Reiki: either *intend* to do this (take your time until you actually feel it expanding outwards) or use Joshin Kokyu-Ho (*see page 129*).

❖ Then sit or stand close enough to the recipient for them to be inside your aura – and simply intend to share Reiki with them.

Other techniques

Mikao Usui is said to have sometimes also used light patting or stroking movements to clear blocked energy. As these techniques count as body manipulation, they are not normally used today. Only a doctor or massage therapist would legally be allowed to use them.

Getting creative

Basically, there's nothing that won't benefit from Reiki. Just play with it – be creative. Here are some suggestions:

Reiki for pets

If you have a pet, I'm sure you love it just as much as I love Lady, my greyhound. And you'll want to give it Reiki too. Well, of course you can!

Lady ran away once in a thunderstorm. The first thing I did was to send Reiki after her with the intention of keeping her safe. Then I started to look for her – initially on foot, then by car (greyhounds are rather fast). I searched for 15 minutes, but there was no trace of her. All I could do was wait (and send more Reiki). Nevertheless I felt strangely calm and somehow knew she would be fine.

Luckily, she was wearing a tag with my phone number on and half an hour later a call came. She had been found – five miles away! She must have crossed many roads – and she doesn't stop at the kerb even when she isn't afraid.

I got her back safely and took her straight to the vet. Her paws were covered in cuts and blisters – the skin was just hanging down. But after three days of Reiki she started running around again – the skin had almost completely healed.

To treat a pet (or in fact any animal), you don't need to follow a particular sequence of hand positions. All you do is intend to give them Reiki when they cuddle up on your lap, or place your hands on or near the area in need.

You may even find that they suddenly come up to you and make you aware that they would like Reiki! One student was completely puzzled when his neighbour's rather frosty cat suddenly came up to him and started to purr. Then it occurred to him that it was sensing his Reiki connection.

If you have a hamster or bird or any other little creature in a cage, you can just place your hands on the outside of the cage to give Reiki. And if you're in a zoo, there's no need to enter the tiger's enclosure. Just beam Reiki from a distance.

Note to professionals
Treating animals professionally is more regulated than treating humans. Please make sure you familiarize yourself with the regulations before you charge for a treatment!

Reiki for plants

One lady told a Reiki Share about a rose bush in a pot that her mother had suggested throwing away as it was 'dead'. After a few days of Reiki (and water, of course) it came back to life. Just like the chilli plant that I rescued from negligence in a supermarket. After two weeks of Reiki it produced chillies on an almost industrial scale. I even put them in scrambled eggs.

You can give Reiki to seeds and indoor plants as well as to fully grown trees or even your entire garden. How do you do that? Just use your imagination – and maybe give Reiki to the watering can...

Reiki for inanimate objects

As we learned earlier, everything is energy, so it follows on that everything can benefit from Reiki. I have given Reiki to my computer and printer (it finished the printing job before it died), car (it lived for three years after being given up on by the local garage) and mobile phone. Currently the dishwasher gets some.

And it even came in handy in convincing a London Underground ticket machine to accept my coins and issue the ticket.

Don't think, *Is it OK to use Reiki for this?* Just do it. Reiki doesn't judge.

Reiki for food

You can give Reiki to the ingredients before you cook, send it while stirring the soup or add it just before serving.

Or you can do the 'purifying water' test: fill two jugs with tap water, give Reiki to one of them for a few minutes and let your guests taste the difference. Reiki seems to harmonize the chemical balance of the water.

Reiki for protection

If you feel you would like to use Reiki to protect yourself from negative energies, there are various visualizations to choose from – or simply use intention.

There are several ways of using intention:

✦ After my Reiki self-treatment, I start every day by intending to be 'guided and guarded by Reiki'. If I feel scared during the day, I'll remember that I've set this intention and feel protected.

✦ Connect to Reiki, feel the connection and then intend to be protected by Reiki, either for the whole day or for a specific situation.

✦ Use *Joshin Kokyu-Ho* to fill your aura with Reiki for protection.

Among the visualizations are:

✦ Draw the Power Symbol (*see page 159*) in front of you, then step into that space, intending that Reiki will protect you.

✦ Visualize yourself being surrounded by a bubble, net or anything else you like as long as it fences you off from the outside world. Connect to Reiki and let it stream out of your palms for a moment, intending that it fills this cocoon around you and protects you.

There are many more visualizations, or you can make up your own. A visualization is simply a way of helping you become aware of the Reiki around you and open up to it.

As mentioned earlier, protection is not necessary for a Reiki treatment.

Reiki for distance healing (after Reiki 1)

Although a proper 'distance treatment' can normally only be given after Reiki 2, even after Reiki 1 you can send Reiki to a person who needs healing.

Think of the person, then write down their name or find a photograph of them. Connect to Reiki and either hold your hands over the name or picture or just 'beam' it to the person you are thinking of.

Reiki for anything and everything

That is exactly how I use Reiki: for anything and everything that comes my way! I give it to an email before I press 'send', to a website before booking a flight, to the plane when I get on board.

Try it out for yourself and see how it works for you...

Reiki for situations

The use of Reiki isn't even restricted to beings or objects – it can also be sent to situations.

Personal situations

Can you think of a personal situation that would benefit from Reiki? It can either be occurring now (your best friend is having a job interview) or in the future (you have to ask your difficult neighbour to lend you their lawn mower).

There are three simple steps:

1. Connect to Reiki (and wait until you feel the connection).

2. Think of (or visualize) the situation.

3. Intend to send Reiki to it.

Alternatively, you can write the situation down (a few words or bullet points are enough), then place your hands over the piece of paper and give it Reiki.

In both cases, send Reiki for as long as you feel a strong sensation in your palms or simply until you feel that you've sent enough. This can take anything from two to 20 minutes but won't normally be longer. After that, stop worrying about it – and let the universe do its work.

Of course the same principle applies as for physical healing: what we wish for may not be the right thing for us. But sending Reiki often works wonders. My own circumstances changed dramatically when Reiki came into my life!

A student of mine was sitting at home one day searching for ideas on how to get further funding for a charity she was involved in. Stuck for inspiration, she decided to give the situation Reiki. She got out the charity's cheque book, placed a leaflet on top detailing all the good work the charity did and placed her hands over it to give it Reiki.

She had just rented out a room in her house and the next evening her new lodger asked her out for a drink so they could get to know each other. Of course my student talked about her involvement in the charity and it turned out that her lodger worked for a big corporation which happened to have its own charitable arm supporting the projects of small charities. It wasn't difficult to come up with an idea for a new project – and two months later the funds arrived. It was the story of the day at the following Reiki Share!

Once you've taken Reiki 2, using the Connection Symbol will greatly increase your ability to connect to situations, as we'll soon see.

World situations

Of course, we don't just face personal problems – the whole world is full of them! So, if you feel guided to do so, you can also send Reiki to world situations.

It works just the same: connect to Reiki, think of the situation and send Reiki there, either through intention or through placing your hands over a picture or article or description of the situation. I occasionally find myself simply sitting in front of the news screen on my computer and sending Reiki to the situation I'm reading about.

Unsurprisingly, it's more difficult to judge the effects of Reiki on such a scale – and we may find the sheer quantity of problems so overwhelming that we don't know where to start and when to stop. It seems to me that first and foremost we are responsible for our immediate environment. Friends, family, neighbours and colleagues are those who can be reached most easily – as well as ourselves, of course. But if you feel guided to send Reiki to a situation on a larger scale, just follow your intuition. I tend to find that we just know when to send Reiki – and when to leave events to unfold.

Occasionally, we might get an idea of the eventual outcome. When I heard about the earthquake in Japan in 2012, the parallels to the one in 1923 were immediately clear. Although, with the epicentre under the sea, it didn't claim as many lives, the effects of the ensuing tsunami, especially on the nuclear power station of Fukushima, had the potential to cause even greater devastation. Every 30 minutes I checked the news on my smartphone – and felt I had to do something. Of course, Reiki was my only tool.

When I started sending Reiki, it was unclear what was going on inside the nuclear reactors. The worst-case scenario that everyone hoped to avoid was a nuclear meltdown due to malfunctioning cooling systems. When I started to connect through Reiki, I suddenly saw that in two reactors the meltdown had already happened. But it was accompanied by a surprising sense of calm, giving me the impression that the consequences could, to a large degree, be contained. A few hours later the news confirmed the meltdown – and over the following weeks it became clear that it had been possible to contain a major outbreak of radiation.

I certainly don't want to claim that this happened because I (and many others as it turned out later) sent Reiki to the situation. And yet, who knows? It certainly was pretty amazing to get a glimpse of the outcome.

Reiki in a group

Reiki need not be a solitary pursuit – practitioners often get together in groups, particularly at Reiki Shares.

Reiki Shares

Many Reiki teachers offer Reiki Shares for their students. These normally consist of a short talk on a Reiki-related subject or a discussion of experiences, a meditation and/or breathing exercises, and often a *Reiju* (energy blessing) from a Reiki Master. This is followed by a group treatment (*see below*).

Reiki Shares are a great way to stay in touch with like-minded people and to share experiences. If your Reiki teacher doesn't organize them, just do it yourself. Get your fellow students together. Or utilize social media. Or search for a Reiki Share in your area.

Group treatment

Exercise: *Shushu* Reiki (Group treatment)

This is where two or more practitioners give Reiki to a person at the same time. They either place their hands on different parts of the body or, if they all feel guided to the same place, one hand on top of the other.

In a very large group, this can be done in circles, with people in the outer circles placing their hands on the shoulders of the people in the circle in front of them.

Exercise: Reiki *Mawashi* (Feeling energy going round a circle)

This technique can be used at a Reiki Share or to increase the awareness of energy whenever a group of Reiki students comes together.

❖ Stand in a circle about 50cm (20 in) away from each other.

❖ Hold your hands horizontally on either side, palm facing up on the right, down on the left. This way, your right hand is underneath your neighbour's left hand and your left hand is on top of your other neighbour's right hand, but not touching.

❖ The teacher puts out the intention to connect to Reiki and starts sending energy out of their left hand.

❖ Feel the energy going round the circle for a while, then change direction.

Quick and Effective

While on the subject of groups, if your friends or colleagues ask you to explain Reiki, frankly I wouldn't even try. After all, I need over 100 pages just to explain the basics. And you would need to cover energy, hands, healing and enlightenment! Instead, simply offer them a taster treatment.

Exercise: A taster treatment

The following hand positions are a great sequence.

❖ Hold your hands in each position for about three minutes, and for the last minute place them on the person's shoulders.

❖ After 10 minutes, they'll have a good idea of what Reiki is. And their headache may have gone too.

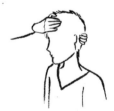  

Head-only treatment

1. Standing beside the client, place one hand on the lower back of their head, the other on the hairline.

2. Now move one hand to the crown and the other to the upper back of the head.

3. Move to stand behind the client and cup your hands over their ears.

SUMMARY

❖ For a Reiki treatment we can either follow a set sequence of hand positions or rely on intuition.

❖ Everyone and everything can benefit from Reiki.

❖ Reiki produces a huge variety of experiences and effects.

Chapter 7

Meditation, breathing, clearing blockages

Mikao Usui made his connection to Reiki after three weeks of fasting and meditating. Fortunately, fasting isn't deemed to be a general part of Reiki practice. Healthy as it is to have a fruit day once a week and generally look after our diet, it isn't essential for Reiki. But meditating very much is.

Oh dear, some readers may be thinking. But those who already meditate will just smile approvingly. They know that meditation is the key to spiritual awareness. Buddha did it, Jesus too (he once retreated to the desert for 40 days). Basically every spiritual master since the beginning of time has done it. But how can we ordinary mortals do it? 'I can't meditate' is probably the complaint most often heard on my Reiki courses. A lot of people struggle with meditation. And I know the feeling very well, as I struggled with it for almost 40 years.

So, before you give up, please let me assure you that the moment you use Reiki, the moment you feel a sensation in your palms and place them on someone, you are meditating. Reiki simply *is* meditation. When we give it, we don't *think*, we *experience*. We move from *doing* to *being*. And the more we let go of our thoughts and ideas, the deeper our connection to Reiki will become.

Out of our mind

In meditation we are free of the constraints of time – and space. We enter a new dimension. Some people experience this as expansion, some as lightness, some as colours or pure light.

As this dimension is beyond what we normally identify with, to reach it we try the opposite of what we are used to; that is, we try to achieve a state of mind that is free of thought. Philosopher René Descartes famously stated, 'I think therefore I am.' When we look at meditation, this statement turns out to be rather superficial. Because even when we don't *think*, we still *are*. We still exist. Not as our everyday selves, but as something deeper.

But how do we get rid of our thoughts? In everyday life, we try so hard to remember things and to work things out, and so often the right thoughts just won't appear. And when we finally give the brain a rest, we're flooded with unwanted thoughts. We try to meditate – and the first thing that comes into our mind is, say, coffee. Where the hell did that come from? Anyway, the thought is there. And it takes us back to the supermarket where we normally do our shopping. Last time, the coffee was out of stock. Thinking about it, quite a few products have been out of stock recently. I wonder if there's a problem with their supply chain. Maybe it's the weather – it is very cold at the moment. Yesterday I stood at the bus stop for 15 minutes almost freezing to death. Why is the bus always late when I'm catching it?

Stop! What's going on here? Am I losing my mind?

No. It's simply going into monkey mode, to use the term of the Eastern meditation traditions, jumping from one thought to the next to the next. I find the best way to deal with this is simply to accept it. Yes, my mind is thinking. So I spend a moment with the thought. It's there. It wants to be acknowledged. But after a few moments I feel I've spent enough time with it and allow it to leave. It has *come* from somewhere – now it can *go* somewhere. I tend to put it into a vehicle that takes it away – a cloud maybe, or a train. This can be whatever you fancy: just imagine it or visualize it, place your thought in it and let it move on.

Then I return to whatever meditation technique I'm using. I may be concentrating on my breath, or on the sensation of Reiki. I find that concentrating on Reiki is much easier than using other techniques, as there is already a strong focal point: the sensation in my palms. But that is only the start. I can now move from concentration to meditation.

To do this, you just have to go in the opposite direction, as it were. You feel the sensation in your hands. But what animates them? Where is the energy coming from? You can actually trace this back! You may feel Reiki flowing through your arms, your shoulders, your head – and trace it back to the crown chakra. Or you may not feel the flow physically, but start to sense that Reiki is, in fact, all around you. And deep inside you. Reiki is ... everywhere. And by opening up to it, you begin to feel that you're everywhere too. You may have a sense of oneness, vastness, expansion. You may start to feel calm, peaceful, free... You may see a light, or brightness.

Making this connection to deeper levels is the ultimate goal of Reiki. We use energy as a means to an end – and become aware of its source.

Here's a step-by-step guide to my ultimate Reiki meditation.

Exercise: My ultimate Reiki meditation

❖ Sit quietly and connect to Reiki.

❖ Place your hands on your thighs, palms up.

❖ Concentrate on the sensations in your palms and become aware of the flow of Reiki through your body. (You can also turn your hands round and rest your palms on your thighs if this makes the sensations stronger.)

❖ Now trace the energy back. Up your arms, then further back. Further still. Wherever your awareness takes you.

You can go deeper and deeper every time you do this. Remember, Reiki works on different levels of the universe and you may be taken to different places at different times. There may even be moments when you feel you're getting close to what Mikao Usui experienced in his moment of enlightenment...

More Reiki meditation techniques

The previous exercise is one I came up with myself. But there are meditation techniques in traditional Reiki too. And they are pleasantly simple...

Seiza

This isn't really a technique – it's the classic Japanese meditation pose. *Seiza* means 'proper sitting'. To sit in *seiza*, you kneel on the floor, resting your bottom on your heels, then turn your ankles outwards so the tops of your feet are on the floor and lower your bottom right down to the floor while keeping your back straight. In Japanese tradition, women keep their knees together and men separate them slightly. Your hands can be folded in your lap, rest palm-down on your thighs or be placed in a half-curl by your hips with your knuckles touching the floor.

This may sound simple, but I have never sat in *seiza* myself. My knees would kill me. Some people use a *seiza* bench in order not to sit directly on their ankles, but even that doesn't work for me. Fortunately, *seiza* isn't necessary. We are allowed to be comfortable in Reiki!

And yet there's often a fine line between comfortable and casual, and a sloppy posture isn't helpful either. The more alert we are and the straighter our spine, the more easily the *ki* can flow. So, by all means sit in *seiza*, or the lotus position, or simply cross-legged, if your physical disposition allows it. In all these cases, your two knees and your buttocks will form a 'tripod', and this is what is important.

If you are more comfortable sitting on a chair, make sure that your feet are placed on the floor (or, if you are too high up, on a cushion or stool), your sitting bones are firmly on the chair and your spine is straight. If you can, I would suggest sitting at the front of the chair and not leaning on the backrest, but this is up to you. You now have the tripod again: a stable base for meditation.

Gassho

Now to meditation techniques. In Reiki, as usual, we start with the hands. Forming *Gassho* is very simple: holding our hands flat, we bring them together, palms and fingers touching, in what is universally known as the prayer position. But there is much more to it than initial observation suggests: it is a traditional way to greet someone, express gratitude and concentrate.

Literally, *Gassho* means 'bringing the hands together', and that is what we do: the left and right meet in the horizontal middle. We find it most comfortable holding them in front of our heart chakra, the vertical middle of our chakras. So we literally *centre* ourselves.

That is the *physical* act. Now comes the awareness.

Normally, we use our hands *physically*. We type or write or draw (or play with our mobile phones). We carry, we lift, we hold. Then we *feel* or *sense* something. We encounter a physical sensation. Often we use our hands independently of each other. Now we can't – we have brought them *together*. We have moved away from work. We have moved away from everyday life. We are holding them *still*.

Looking at the hands in *Gassho*, we first thing we may realize is that we tend to hold them with the fingers pointing upwards. They are pointing *away* from the Earth. Away from our *physical* selves. They are pointing towards heaven.

Next we may realize that we have brought the two hands *together*. But *what* did we bring together? First, *left* and *right*. Our two halves.

Looking at our brain and imagining our hands being guided by it, being an *extension* of it, we may realize that we've brought the two sides of our being together: the left brain, our intellect, controlling how we function in the world, and the right brain, the centre of our intuition, emotions and spiritual awareness, where we find guidance and peace.

There is a common saying that when people appear slightly confused, 'the right hand doesn't know what the left hand is doing'. In *Gassho* the hands do know. They are held together. They are in the *same* place.

Having brought our attention to the position of our hands in the centre between left and right (or, rather, transcending left and right), we can now look vertically. The heart chakra doesn't just represent the centre of the chakra system but also the centre of the Three Diamonds system. Below is the *Hara*, the seat of Earth energy, connecting us with the level of form. Above is the third eye, the seat of the heaven energy, connecting us to the world of spirit.

So, by holding our hands in the *Gassho* position, we bring all aspects of our person into harmony. From this point, we can reach out. The *Centre Diamond*, the heart, is the place of connection, the place where we feel love, harmony and peace. We can now fully focus on being at one – with everybody and everything, and with our own true self.

Exercise: *Gassho* meditation (Bringing the hands together)

❖ Sit comfortably in *seiza* or the lotus position or cross-legged or on a chair. Straighten your spine.

❖ Connect to Reiki.

❖ Bring your hands together in the prayer position in front of your heart chakra.

❖ Focus on your hands.

Gassho

There are several versions of *Gassho*. You may also want to try moving your hands higher up, with the fingertips just below the brow chakra. It helps to focus on the third eye - and your connection to spirit.

Joshin Kokyu-Ho

Joshin Kokyu-Ho is deep abdominal breathing. If you practise yoga, it will be familiar to you; if not, it will feel strange. But you'll soon get used to it! An amazing technique, it's nonetheless the opposite of what we're used to: rather than breathing into our chest, we breathe into our *belly*.

Between the stomach and the lungs we find a muscle called the diaphragm. It is attached to both stomach and lungs, which means that the movement of one affects the other. We utilize this in this exercise, where we move the stomach out and therefore pull the lungs down. This allows us to breathe into the full depth of the lungs.

A great exercise in itself, this can also be used to focus the mind, clear the meridians and strengthen and connect to the energy in the *Hara*. In Reiki, however, we go one step further and use the breath as a vehicle to open up to universal energy.

Exercise: *Joshin Kokyu-Ho* (Deep abdominal breathing)

❖ Sit on a chair, or cross-legged, or in *seiza* or the lotus position on the floor, keeping your spine straight.

❖ If you wish, you may place your hands in the *Gassho* position to centre your mind.

❖ Then bring your hands to your lap or knees and let them rest there, palms up. (To begin with, you can also place them on your belly to support and feel the *Hara*.)

❖ Breathe in through your nose and deeply into your lungs. As you use your diaphragm to pull the air in, let your stomach expand outwards. Concentrate on the sensation of the air coming in through your nose and filling your lungs. Once the lower parts of your lungs have been filled, you will notice that your diaphragm will relax slightly.

❖ Carry on filling the middle and upper parts of your lungs. You should breathe slowly, taking up to eight seconds for an in-breath.

❖ For the out-breath, use your stomach as a pump and gently squeeze out the air until your lungs are completely empty. Breathing in and out should take equal amounts of time.

❖ Now intend to connect to Reiki and to use the breath as a vehicle to bring it in.

❖ Breathing in deeply, intend or visualize that you are breathing in Reiki.

❖ Breathing out, intend or visualize that the energy is expanding through your whole body and even beyond, into your aura.

❖ Breathing slowly and deeply, continue this exercise for several minutes. You can go on for up to 15 minutes if you wish. Be sure to stop if you feel dizzy. You can extend the time gradually as you continue your practice.

❖ You may want to finish by placing your hands in the Gassho position and thanking Reiki.

With experience, you will become aware of the energy slowly building up in your body. You should feel refreshed and more energetic throughout the day and may also be more grounded and centred.

Energy cleansing

When the original Reiki teachings became known to a wider audience, most of the above had not been practised. Nor had there been any energy cleansing rituals – and yet Reiki still worked. This confirms once again that Reiki is not about techniques.

Introducing energy cleansing, though, makes a lot of sense. Blockages in our energy system can occur all the time, triggered by factors such as stress, worry or anger, but also by an unhealthy diet or lifestyle, lack of sleep, etc. Energy cleansing helps to clear the blockages and lets the energy flow fast and freely. It brings us right into the moment.

The technique used here was introduced by Mikao Usui, but not invented by him. In fact it is widely used in martial arts.

Kenyoku-Ho (Dry bathing)

Kenyoku-Ho means 'dry bathing'. It sounds far more complicated than it actually is. You simply make a few swift movements through your energy body with the intention of clearing any blockages. Once you're used to it, it will only take a few seconds to complete.

This is how it goes:

Exercise: *Kenyoku-Ho* (Dry bathing)

❖ Breathing in (take a normal breath, not the deep abdominal version), bring your right hand to your left shoulder.

❖ Breathing out, take your right hand down towards your right hip in one swift diagonal movement.

- ❖ Breathing in, bring your left hand to your right shoulder.

- ❖ Breathing out, take your left hand diagonally down to your left hip.

- ❖ Breathing in, bring your right hand up to your left shoulder again.

- ❖ Breathing out, bring your hand diagonally down to your right hip again.

- ❖ Now stretch your left arm out in front of you, palm up.

- ❖ Breathing in, bring your right hand to your left shoulder.

- ❖ Breathing out, move your hand swiftly along your left arm from the shoulder to the palm.

- ❖ Stretch your right arm out in front of you, palm up.

- ❖ Breathing in, bring your left hand to your right shoulder.

- ❖ Breathing out, move your hand swiftly along your right arm from the shoulder to the palm.

- ❖ Now stretch your left arm out again, palm up.

- ❖ Breathing in, bring your right hand to your left shoulder again.

- ❖ Breathing out, move your hand swiftly along your left arm again, from the shoulder to the palm.

While making the movements, your hands may be touching your body slightly or may be kept off.

If you do the exercise quickly, you may find it easier to take a deep breath in at the beginning then breathe out slowly while you do all the dry brushing.

And yes, you do indeed cleanse the left side twice and the right only once – a concession to the Japanese tradition (or superstition) of avoiding anything that includes the number four. In Japanese, it is the same word as the one for death.

Kenyoku-Ho can also be used after a treatment or meditation to bring you back into the here and now. It is a great technique for grounding yourself.

Reiki shower

Another technique, although not an original one, is the so-called Reiki shower. It works brilliantly when you're tired or feel burdened by negative energy, for example at work, after a long day shopping or when watching the news on TV. You can also use it instead of *Kenyoku-Ho* before you give a Reiki treatment.

Exercise: Reiki shower

❖ Connect to Reiki.

❖ Raise your hands above your head, one on top of the other, palms facing down.

❖ Intend or ask Reiki to stream down from this 'showerhead' over your body and through your aura, then move your hands down in front of your body to 'remove' any released energy.

❖ Repeat this twice.

❖ Finish by placing your hands in *Gassho*.

A cold shower

In many ascetic esoteric traditions, the monks will stand under an ice-cold waterfall – for 30 minutes. Even in winter. Personally, I can't see myself doing this – even the English sea in August is too cold for me.

A great and more accessible modern take on this is simply to have a cold shower! I do this every morning for about 10 seconds, intending that it will clear my meridians and chakras and get rid of any negative energy. And it works – sometimes I have to rush out of the shower because I've just had a new idea. Standing under cold running water (even if only in agreeable doses) is a great way of seeing things more clearly.

Afterwards, of course, I have a nice warm relaxing shower.

Bringing it all together: *Hatsurei-Ho*

Now it's time to bring it all together. Put simply, *Hatsurei-Ho*, 'purifying the energy' or 'purifying the spirit', is a combination of the cleansing, breathing and *Gassho* that can deepen our connection to Reiki. In fact, it can help us get so deep that there is no boundary between us and Reiki and we become *one* with the universe.

There are several versions of this in Japan and it seems that many Reiki teachers have come up with their own versions too. This is the basic one that I use:

Exercise: *Hatsurei-Ho* (Purifying the energy)

❖ Start with *Kenyoku-ho* (dry bathing).

❖ Connect to Reiki, feel the flow and then spend 5–10 minutes using *Joshin Kokyu-Ho* (deep abdominal breathing): Place your hands on your thighs, palms facing up, intend to breathe in Reiki and then let it flow through your physical and energy bodies when you breathe out.

❖ Now bring your hands together in Gassho (in front of your heart chakra) and shift your awareness to your hands.

❖ Continuing to breathe deeply, imagine that Reiki is now entering your heart chakra straight from your palms – as if you were breathing *through* your palms...

❖ When you breathe out, you can visualize Reiki flowing into every part of your body, into your aura and into the environment.

To start with, you may find it helpful to visualize the flow and expansion of Reiki as light. But after a while you'll be able to let go of this and simply *feel* Reiki.

SUMMARY

❖ In meditation we go beyond what can be grasped with the five senses.

❖ Practising Reiki is a form of meditation.

❖ Breathing and cleansing exercises are part of the original teachings and help us to open up more to Reiki.

Chapter 8

Principles and poetry: bringing the light into everyday life

Do we really need more principles in this world? As we have seen, Reiki isn't about content but awareness. It certainly isn't about rules. Why then principles?

Because life isn't easy! Mikao Usui was well aware that his students would continue to have normal lives, with jobs, families and everyday challenges. The system already reflects this – we aren't asked to do anything that isn't compatible with everyday life. And yet what do you do with your healing hands if you have a difficult boss? How do you keep up with your breathing and meditation exercises when you do shift work and spend most of your time off asleep? Do you give yourself a Reiki treatment to calm yourself down when you've missed the bus?

This is where the Reiki principles come in: they help us to live in Reiki awareness all the time. They allow us to practise oneness. And they clear more of the blockages that stand between us and Reiki.

The Reiki principles

A frosty start

If you're like me, you've heard (and possibly tried to follow) so many principles, rules, regulations, moral codes and ideas on how to change your behaviour that you are, frankly, sick of them. Thank you for the moral high ground, but we have normal life to contend with. Please stop the theory – I want something I can apply!

This is how I started (or rather *didn't* start) with the Reiki principles. I heard them and discarded them.

It didn't help that I wasn't given the correct principles. Instead, mine included a paragraph asking me to honour my teachers and elders – and I'd had challenging experiences with teachers and elders in my life.

If you've come across a similar version of the Reiki principles, rest assured they're not original. I assume the offending paragraph was added by a Reiki teacher having a bad day.

The real Reiki principles are at the very heart of the original Reiki teachings. They are given a lot of space on the memorial stone and it is suggested that they're repeated *every day*. By doing so, you may find what I eventually found for myself: they are utterly, utterly helpful. I cannot do without them any more. I would go as far as to state that they have transformed my life.

This is a translation[1] of the original version from the memorial stone:

Just for today,
Do not be angry.
Do not worry.
Be grateful.
Do your work with diligence.
Be kind to others.

Let's start with three interesting observations:

1. There are only five principles

No sub-clauses, no hidden meanings. This is important, because it is just as much as most people can handle. Our conscious mind is easily overworked. Then it gets stressed – and forgets. And what is forgotten cannot be applied. If we go to the corner shop to get some milk, it's an easy task. If our partner asks us to get some eggs as well, we're able to handle it. If the kids want some chocolate, and perhaps apples, we start to panic. Or at least we need to write it all down. Just imagine what would happen if the telephone number for emergency services had seven digits instead of three. Plus the area code. Hospitals would only deal with corpses.

Five principles are what we can remember. And therefore apply.

2. They are simple

Very simple, in fact. We're so used to having philosophical ideas crafted in the most sophisticated and elaborate sentences, often tapping into the pool of rarely used foreign words, that we almost feel that something plain and simple cannot have much depth. But the principles are carefully worded. They avoid words like 'Oneness', 'Buddhahood' or 'Emptiness', which trigger an intellectual discourse (although, if you're a spiritual scholar, you'll find that in essence the meaning is not so different). And we don't need to waste energy in trying to make sense of them. We can fully concentrate on their *application*.

3. There is no punishment attached

Principles or rules of conduct are found in every religion and on every spiritual path. Often they are linked to a system of punishment. This may range from the threat of being reborn as a fly (or at least a member of a lower caste) to ending up in eternal hell. In German there is a saying: 'Small sins God punishes straight away.' This is normally applied when someone has told a lie or backed out of giving a helping hand and then slipped on a banana skin lying on the pavement or the lie has been uncovered immediately, to much embarrassment.

The Reiki principles take a completely different approach. They are based on the understanding that they are *good for you*. Nothing else. If you apply them, it will be good for you; if you don't apply them, you are missing an opportunity to feel better. It's up to you. There is no punishment – just a missed opportunity. And you haven't even missed it forever. Not even for long. You can simply try again. Straight away.

Repeat, repeat, repeat

In the Japanese tradition, the principles are regarded as a key to opening up to Reiki. Mikao Usui referred to them as 'the secret method to invite happiness' and the 'miraculous medicine to cure all diseases'.[2] He asked his students to sit in *Gassho* and repeat them every morning and every evening.

So, repeat them again and again and again. Use auto-hypnosis. Say them, think them, dream them. Become them.

Whenever you need them, you want them to be the first thing to pop into your mind. The conscious mind is forgetful, so you want to really imprint these principles into the subconscious. Just like driving a car. When a car stops in front of you, you automatically hit the brake. You don't reflect a while and then tell yourself, 'Considering all options, braking now would be the most beneficial.' By then the airbag will have inflated.

The Reiki principles are tools to *train* the mind. They add an element of psychology to Reiki and work on conscious and subconscious levels.

It would be easy to fill an entire book with the many layers of the principles, but for now I will just concentrate on a few key aspects. You will find out more by applying them.

Just for today

Mother Teresa had a fabulous hands-on approach: 'We have only today. Let us begin.' This is what this introduction to the principles encourages us to do: *begin*. Implement the principles. Don't wait!

There's no excuse. If we look carefully, we *have* got the time. The American Lama Surya Das says: '...it's not time we lack, but focus, priorities, and awareness.'[3] Having the time or not is a matter of choice.

'Just for today' also means: 'I may have tried yesterday, I may not have always succeeded yesterday, but yesterday is gone. Today is another day, another chance, and I will try again. Again and again, until I succeed.'

Every day is a blank sheet, and step by step, we improve.

Do not be angry

When I discuss this principle on a Reiki course, the reaction isn't always positive. We seem to be hugely resistant to either accepting or confronting anger. Quite a few people have suggested rewording the principle. They would prefer to repeat 'I am calm' or 'I am peaceful' or 'I am relaxed.'

Simply repeating 'Do not be angry' can make us feel uncomfortable. The negative phrasing brings up anger rather than suppressing it. But that is exactly what it is designed to do! This principle isn't an affirmation. It isn't designed to airbrush, suppress or negate anger – it's meant to bring it up! In order to deal with it, we need to be aware of it.

After repeating 'Do not be angry' a few times, a student of mine once started crying. Memories of a huge confrontation with her mother flashed up – from 15 years before! She was shocked to find that this incident was still so ingrained in her subconscious that a simple exercise could bring it up. But Reiki had finally brought her the strength to deal with it.

Harbouring anger is never beneficial, either for the person holding on to it (it makes us both miserable and ill) or for the person at whom it is eventually directed. The Buddha concluded: 'You will not be punished for your anger; you will be punished by your anger.'

The principle does not say: 'Handle your anger.' Nor: 'Share your anger.' It says: 'Do not *be* angry.' Which means: 'Be something *else*.' It reminds us that we have a choice.

Anger is triggered by disappointment, shock, insecurity – or just being interrupted. We were expecting something that turned out to be different. So what happens then?

The chemicals that are subsequently released and that make us 'feel' anger are dealt with by the body quite quickly. They are completely flushed out of our system in less than 90 seconds.[4] All we need to do is take a deep breath and hold on for a minute – and our response to the situation doesn't need to be directed by anger, but by whatever we choose to replace it with.

Can we change the situation? Can we change our attitude? Learn for next time? Accept? Forgive?

Or, maybe, take action? Does our anger lead us to make the world a better place?

Now anger turns into something useful: a tool for change. And there's no need to hold on to it.

This Reiki principle offers the opportunity to react differently.

Do not worry

During the years between my bankruptcy and my discovery of Reiki, a friend once asked me if I had a wish for the New Year. I said, 'To wake up one morning without fear.' So for

143

me to write about 'Do not worry' is like being a bank robber advertising burglar alarms. But a recovering one. Reiki gradually brought help. And with it trust.

Worries are nothing but lack of trust: 'Last time something difficult happened, so it might happen again tomorrow!' Well, it might. Or it might not. If it does, we need to deal with it. Tomorrow. Not today. If it doesn't, our worries will have been a complete waste of time. I'm sure I wasted years of my life worrying.

If worries lead to proper preparation, they have served their purpose. We can let them go and leave the rest to the universe. And we can send Reiki to the problem. It's easier said than done, of course. Everyone goes through difficult phases and sometimes they seem to last forever. But they don't. One day they will have passed.

And the more we let go of our worries, the more we open to synchronicity. And miracles.

Be grateful

A while ago this principle was the topic of a Reiki Share – and we did a practical exercise too. Every participant was asked to write down five things they were grateful for. Some started writing straight away, some took a moment to do an inner search, but afterwards almost everyone complained that five weren't enough – they'd found so many more!

The good old gratefulness list is a brilliant tool to make us aware that there *are* things we're grateful for. We just have a tendency to casually overlook them (the famous glass-half-empty attitude).

Once we realize we *are* grateful, we can often feel an almost physical sensation in our whole body. Our energy becomes the happy vibration of gratitude.

A student mentioned that while giving a Reiki treatment once she was overwhelmed by gratitude for the connection. As soon as this came in, the heat in her hands tripled. Gratefulness is an incredible tool for clearing blockages.

Do your work with diligence

When I first heard this principle, it sounded odd. What is spiritual about focusing on your work? It took a while before it dawned on me that it wasn't just about work, it was about our whole life.

Whatever we do, whatever situation we are in, we need to act with diligence. In contemporary language, this means we need to take responsibility for our life. Where we are may not be our choice, but how we act definitely is.

We are never in the wrong place, in fact: we are where the universe placed us. No matter whether we know it or not, we are here for a purpose. We can make the most of it if we apply three basic ideas. Mindfulness. Respect. Honesty.

This applies to having a shave in the morning (today I did mine in a rush, and currently sport a little cut), to listening to the person we are having a conversation with (my sister recently noticed that I wasn't giving her my undivided attention on the phone), and to carrying out our job. Basically, every task will improve if we do it with diligence.

And, of course, the more diligent we are with Reiki itself, the more it can change our lives.

Be kind to others

I once took part in an exercise at a spiritual seminar. Paired up with somebody we hardly knew, or even a complete stranger, we were asked to give them a compliment. First there was a moment of silence – most of us didn't know quite what to do. Then people began to 'positively examine' their partner. The first person came out with: 'Cool shoes.' Then it was: 'Nice glasses.' 'You have beautiful eyes.' 'Do you know that you have an amazing smile?' 'I admire your courage, coming on this course on your own.' A few minutes later, the room was filled with happy people. The entire energy had changed.

Kindness doesn't have to be difficult. It can be offering your spare bedroom to a friend (as happened to me when I lost my home – thank you, Ari and Bob!); it can be offering a smile to the cashier in the supermarket. And of course Reiki is an amazing tool for sharing kindness.

An excellent book by David Hamilton, *Why Kindness is Good for You*, examines the most recent worldwide research into kindness and draws some amazing conclusions. Research at various universities has shown that people who do the highest number of acts of kindness also score highest in terms of personal happiness. The act of giving leads to more fulfilment than the act of receiving. And, interestingly, it is through emotional warmth that the hormone *oxytocin* is produced. Lining the arteries in our body, this is vital in preventing cardiovascular disease. Dr Hamilton concludes that being kind leads to health and happiness.

Every day is full of opportunities to show kindness. And full of opportunities to do the opposite. This Reiki principle reminds us that the choice is ours.

Exercise: Reciting the principles

I would strongly recommend following Mikao Usui's advice. Every morning and every evening, sit for a moment in *Gassho* and repeat the principles.

But please take your time. I sometimes stop suddenly halfway through and think: *You didn't mean it!* And start again: 'Just for today, I will not be angry [then I pause for a moment and check whether I'm holding anger or feelings of resentment], I will not worry [pause again: *Am I worrying? Have I given my worries over to Reiki?*], I will be grateful [pause again to see what comes up], I will do my work with diligence [where do I need to improve?] and I will be kind to others [anyone in particular today?].'

It's phenomenal!

Exercise: Repeating the principles

I learned this exercise from Reiki Master Frans Stiene and find it exceptionally powerful.

❖ Sit in meditation posture (*see pages 125–6*).

❖ Start with *Kenyoku-Ho* (*page 131*).

❖ Connect to Reiki.

❖ Place your hands either on your thighs, palms up, or in *Gassho*.

❖ Repeat a Reiki principle for five minutes, or longer if you wish. Choose whichever seems appropriate. If you are worried, use 'I will not worry', etc.

❖ Stop repeating it and spend a few minutes observing how you feel.

❖ Place your hands in *Gassho* to thank Reiki.

I would only repeat one Reiki principle at a time.

Waka poetry

Mikao Usui – and then Dr Hayashi and the Reiki Gakkai – also used a second element of content in the system of Reiki: Waka poetry, which is a particular form of short poetry. The Meiji emperor wrote over 100,000 of these poems in his life and his wife added another 40,000.

As Waka poems often touch on spirituality, ethical conduct and personal development, Usui gave a booklet of 125 of them to each of his students. The main intention was to give them a tool for personal reflection and inspiration, but it may also have served another (rather smart) purpose: to make sure that the imperial authorities didn't consider the system of Reiki at all suspicious.

Today, most of these poems sound a bit outdated, and a certain degree of knowledge of 19th-century Japanese culture is necessary to understand them fully. As far as I am aware, hardly anybody uses them any more.

Instead, we can view this idea as encouragement to further our intellectual understanding of spiritual concepts. For many students, Reiki is the start of a long learning process that involves spiritual books. I tend to find that we are guided to the ones that are right for us.

Staying in the spirit of short inspirations, many people nowadays use card decks with quotes. I also use bibliomancy: I ask for guidance and then open a book at random, reading just one sentence or paragraph. This can be done with books by great spiritual authors like Eckhart Tolle, Neale Donald Walsch or Thich Nhat Hanh, or even works of literature (it is amazing what Shakespeare still has to say, I find). And, of course, it can be done with religious scriptures.

SUMMARY

* The Reiki principles are designed to bring the Reiki awareness into everyday life.

* They should be repeated every day until they automatically pop up in any situation where they are required.

* Waka poetry reminds us that we should make use of spiritual texts for contemplation and reflection.

Chapter 9
Okuden/Reiki 2: Shining brighter

Everything covered over the last 100 pages relates to Reiki 1. (It's amazing how much is possible after just a two-day course!) It's perfectly fine to remain on this level. We can use Reiki for ourselves, and others, and basically give it to everything we feel could benefit from it. We can open up more by using meditation, breathing and cleansing techniques. And we have principles to apply in our everyday life. What can possibly be added by Reiki 2?

Well, a lot, actually. I often hear that students find Reiki 2 an even bigger step than Reiki 1. The first course introduces something *new*. No matter what we've done before, we're all beginners when it comes to learning Reiki. It's for that reason that it's called *Shoden* in Japanese: 'the beginner's level'. Reiki 2 is called *Okuden*: 'the deeper teachings'. And this is what we do now: go deeper. Now we have our connection to universal energy, we can explore what the universe is all about.

Symbols

No more myths

The main tools for this exploration are the famous Reiki symbols. But to use them properly, we first need to demystify them.

For many decades, these symbols were either called sacred or secret, or often both – terms normally used to scare people, or at least keep them away. What was the reason for it? I assume a simple one: these words tend to be used to deflect from our own lack of knowledge. When something is secret or sacred, we don't need to explain it...

I would like to take the myths away. The symbols are neither secret (certainly not in the age of the internet) nor sacred. They are man-made. They serve a purpose. They are simply tools created by Mikao Usui to help us see *more*: they help us to concentrate on different aspects of Reiki. And, as always in Reiki, they don't just point to theory but to *experience*.

However, one thing needs to be conceded to those who try to keep the symbols secret: they are only of use once we've been attuned to them. Without the attunement, they are nothing but decorative drawings. So, as much as I am opposed to any form of secrecy, there is no need to publicize the symbols widely to people who don't practise Reiki.

And yet (to demolish another myth), they will do no harm in uninitiated hands. Absolutely not! It is impossible to do anything bad with Reiki, or with the Reiki symbols.

What are symbols?

A symbol is a representation of something *else*. It's never about the symbol itself, it's always about what it points to. The dollar sign ($), for instance, is a symbol. And (unfortunately) we cannot buy anything with it. All it does is make us aware that the product it is attached to doesn't come for free. It is exchanged for money, it has a price. The power doesn't lie in the symbol, but in our purse.

Or take the Eiffel Tower. Does anyone looking at it ever think of the World Fair that it was erected for in 1889? Or of the remarkable technical effort needed to construct what was then the tallest man-made structure in the world? Probably not. Most people simply think of Paris. The building has become a symbol of the city – the most romantic city in the world! People think of Edith Piaf, *chansons* and romantic dinners. So the Eiffel Tower has become a symbol of love and romance. Here, as so often, the meaning isn't apparent in the symbol itself, but lies in the associations we ourselves have made.

The same applies to the Reiki symbols. Teaching his system to a variety of people, Usui noticed huge differences in their ability to feel and understand Reiki. Everybody got healing hands, but when it came to sensing subtle differences in the energy, only a few were able to do it naturally. For the others, he designed the symbols as concentration tools for meditation and applying Reiki practically. And (to eliminate yet another myth), he didn't rediscover ancient symbols. Two of those he used were already part of different Buddhist traditions and the other two he made up himself.

The fact that a student needs to be attuned in order to use the symbols shows where the real power lies: in the attunement. In Reiki. Not in the symbol.

The concept behind the Reiki symbols

The symbols help us to understand the structure of the universe and our own place in it. And then to make the most of it!

Finally grasping this concept was a big turning-point in my view of Reiki. It moved from being a complementary therapy to a complete philosophical system. The real magnificence of what it allows us to understand started to shine through.

Few books have included this concept yet, as research has only recently brought it to light. So if you've been practising Reiki for a while, even if you're a Reiki Master, you may not have come across it. What I love about it is that it makes sense. In fact, I feel that it is only in the light of this concept that the system of Reiki makes complete sense.

The ideas Mikao Usui utilized were well known in his time in Japan. Based on Taoist teachings, they formed the basis of the flower-arranging art of ikebana, as well as a variety of cultural and philosophical traditions. But through Reiki, they moved from theoretical to tangible.

As we've already seen, the universe (or cosmos) is a macrocosm – and our body a micro version of it. The fact that the universe and our individual existence are connected means, in turn, that everybody is connected. With Reiki (universal energy), we are tapping into the power of this interconnectedness.

From our perspective within the universe (in the Master level we go even further and take a step beyond), we can distinguish between three levels: the level of form, the level of spirit and the level of oneness. Fascinatingly, even down here on the level of form it's possible to experience them all.

In creating the symbols to grasp this connection, Usui did such a good job that they even work for people who don't know anything of the theory behind them. But together with this awareness, they can open up a whole new world.

The size of this book restricts a very deep exploration of the symbols, which could easily fill an entire book. For now, though, I feel the following pages will give a sufficiently good idea of what the symbols stand for – and how their use can make an enormous difference.

The elements of the Reiki symbols

We all learn, remember and even sense in different ways – some visual, some auditory, some intellectual. With this in mind, Mikao Usui incorporated three facets into these learning tools:

1. Drawing

The visual representation, or simply shape. Using either a finger or your whole hand, you normally draw the symbol in the air in front of you. Another way is to draw or visualize it in your mind. Most people do this when they concentrate on their third eye chakra. In the Western tradition, drawing the symbol is accompanied by repeating its mantra (*see below*) three times.

2. The mantra

A mantra is a sequence of *kanji* evoking the same qualities as the symbol. As mentioned earlier, *kanji* are logographic characters that represent a word or a syllable. Imported from China about 2,000 years ago, until the early 20th century they made up the entire Japanese language. After the Second World War many of them were simplified or replaced and new characters added. Each has an individual meaning, but together they reveal a deeper message.

A mantra is normally used in connection with the respective symbol, but also works on its own. It is repeated three times and can be said either silently or aloud.

3. Kotodama

A *kotodama* uses vowels to create a certain energetic vibration. In the system of Reiki the vowels contained in the mantras are used. A *kotodama* can be chanted silently or aloud. Neither a good singing voice nor a particular note is necessary, so no excuses – *chanting* is *not* singing!

The idea behind the *kotodama* is the notion that words and sounds *carry energy*.

Initially, the use of any of these elements will feel a bit odd. You draw an elaborate sign with your fingers, repeat foreign words and chant vowels – what are you doing?! But just wait for the effect. It is mind-blowing. Very soon using these elements will be second nature.

Here are three practical tips for drawing the symbols:

1. Make sure that you *learn them properly*. Draw them again and again until you're satisfied that you know them by heart. That way you won't worry about how to draw them and can concentrate on the sensation of their energy. In the beginning you can draw them on a piece of paper and place it next to you when you want to use them.

2. You will discover that your hands have a fabulous new function: *a built-in eraser*. If you aren't sure whether the symbol you've drawn is correct, simply erase it and start again. Even seasoned Reiki practitioners do this.

3. If you draw a symbol incorrectly, you may not feel its energy as strongly. But that is the only effect it can have. *It is impossible to attract other (even negative) energies* when we make a mistake with a symbol. After all, we're using it in our connection to Reiki – and the *intention* is the overriding factor.

The symbols are a means to an end. The more we use them, the more we open up to the different levels of our existence in the universe. One day we may be so open that the symbols have served their purpose – and we can discard them. Japanese Reiki teacher Hiroshi Doi, an ex-member of the Gakkai Training organization, refers to the symbols as 'training wheels'. They are helpful to get us going, but aren't needed when we're up and running. Frankly, though, it is very rare to be skilled enough to use Reiki entirely without them. Personally, I don't know anybody who does. For most practitioners, the symbols will be an important part of their practice throughout their life.

The Power Symbol

Meaning

The Power Symbol (sometimes also called the Focus Symbol) represents *Earth energy*. Once we internalize this idea, we'll have no problems deciding when to use it. It helps to bring Reiki to the level of form: our life in the here and now. Although in essence we are spiritual beings, while we are incarnated in a body we have corresponding needs. Our body needs to function, and we depend on food and drink, income and home. When there's a problem, Reiki is at hand – in the shape of Earth energy.

As we have already noted, the energy centre in the body where we hold Earth energy is the *Hara*, the *lower* Tanden or *navel chakra*. In many Eastern energy traditions, this is seen as the centre of our life-force energy. Focusing on building up energy here can significantly improve our physical strength and wellbeing.

Visual representation

The spiral is used in many spiritual traditions. It has been found on Sanskrit, Celtic and ancient Egyptian artefacts, among others. When we look at a spiral it often 'comes to life', starting to spin and drawing us into its centre. But Mikao Usui added two more lines when he created this Reiki symbol, which means that, contrary to information given elsewhere, the symbol does not seem to be plucked from other traditions, but custom-made for Reiki.

I like the following interpretation: the first, horizontal, line signifies the manifestation of energy – an object or a situation is created. The vertical line then goes straight inside this creation. Finally, we just concentrate on the problem ... and circle into the centre of what needs Reiki.

The anticlockwise movement may symbolize that Reiki can *change* a situation – just as a screw is turned in this direction when it is in the wrong place and we want to *undo* it. What had been stuck is loosened – and can be recreated.

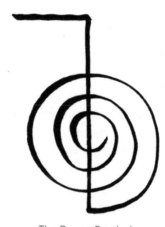

The Power Symbol

Mantra

CHO KU REI (pronounced 'Chow Koo Ray')

As the meaning of individual *kanji* tends to change with context, we will only look at the translation of these three *kanji* together. *Cho Ku Rei* can best be translated as 'direct spirit'. It cuts through the form and brings in spirit.

Kotodama

O-U-E-I (pronounced 'Ow ooh ayh eee')

The *kotodama* has no intellectual meaning – it simply carries energy. Even if you haven't learned this on your Reiki course, I would suggest sitting quietly for a moment (and closing the doors, otherwise your family may think you have become a bit odd), taking a deep breath and then chanting: *'O ... U ... E ... I.'*

Do this for a few minutes and then observe how you feel. It's a great way to sense the energetic vibration.

Use

The Power Symbol is surely the most often-used symbol in Reiki. I don't think a day passes when I don't use it at least 10 or 20 times. It helps to bring Reiki into the here and now – and that's always needed! I sometimes just seem to be walking around '*Cho-Ku-Rei*-ing' everything: a dying plant, a cut or bruise, my computer, my car, my dinner in a restaurant, a plane before take-off, the ingredients before cooking. It brings strength, focus and energy, and many people use it for protection and space clearing.

Often, Reiki practitioners draw the Power Symbol on their palms before giving a treatment. It feels as if they are turning into a Teflon pan with a red-hot dot in the middle just radiating energy!

During a treatment, whenever an energy blockage or a physical problem is detected, you may either draw the Power Symbol over the area or (silently) chant the *kotodama*.

The Harmony Symbol

Meaning

The Harmony Symbol represents *heaven energy*. And again, once we understand the concept behind it, it's easy to determine when to use it. It deals with our mind, our emotions and our connection to the spirit realm – everything we cannot grasp with our five senses, yet are very much aware is there (and if we aren't, Reiki will make sure that we *become* aware).

It helps us to realize that we're not on our own. We can always ask for help, guidance and insight from the 'other side'. And it works on issues of the mind, bringing harmony and balance and dealing with trauma and negativity.

The energy centre for heaven energy is the *third eye*: the *upper* Tanden or *brow chakra*. Many Reiki students even feel a physical sensation when it is activated (but it works anyway, whether we are aware of it or not).

Visual representation

When Usui searched for a concentration tool representing heaven energy, he was reminded of the religious teachings of his childhood. They must have been a pleasant memory, as he decided to use the symbol for Pure Land Buddhism's main deity: Amida Nyorai. He represents the heavenly aspects of love, compassion, grace, harmony and forgiveness, and is often called the Buddha of Infinite Light. Usui seems to have slightly streamlined the drawing to bring it into line with the way the other symbols were drawn.

The Harmony Symbol

Mantra

SEI HEKI (pronounced 'Say Heh-kee')

Together, the *kanji* of *Sei HeKi* can be translated as 'natural tendency', 'mental habit' or (as they are most often translated) 'bad habit'. And we have quite a few bad habits! Being out of balance, negative or lonely. Not seeing or seeking guidance from the spirit world. Identifying only with our physical body. However, a bit like the first two Reiki principles, repeating the negative helps us to realize these are misconceptions and go beyond them. (*See also page 142.*)

A little warning:
Times change, and so does language. Please note that in contemporary Japanese the expression *Sei HeKi* has taken on a new meaning and is now associated with certain sexual

practices – or even used as a synonym for 'perverted'. (I would therefore not suggest walking around Tokyo and shouting this at people.)

Kotodama

E-I-E-KI (pronounced 'Ayh eee ayh kee')

Use

It took me a while to relate to this symbol. Its energy felt so much subtler than that of the Power Symbol that I hardly noticed it. In time, though, I was able to feel it much more strongly – so please keep on using this symbol and don't be disappointed by a potentially slow beginning. I am sure you'll eventually see extraordinary results!

The Harmony Symbol is used for the following:

❖ Connecting to the spirit realm (guides, angels and family members in spirit). You may suddenly become aware of a presence and will be able to feel their warmth, love and help.

❖ Increasing intuition. Just ask and you'll suddenly 'know'.

❖ Supporting creativity and artistic expression. Whether you paint, write, design or cook, you'll be inspired.

❖ Bringing harmony and balance – the natural result of focusing on spirit!

❖ Helping with relationship issues. Time for a talk? Time to get closer again? (*See also page 199.*)

❖ Dealing with addictions and negative habits. It doesn't have to be class A drugs – I'm sure we all have areas in our life where we need help with this.

Heaven energy can also be used to help overcome depression. In fact I'm certain that Reiki could significantly reduce the dangerous (and scarily widespread) habit of prescribing anti-depressants. (Sorry, pharmaceutical industry, but I really think you've got it wrong there.)

Occasionally, Reiki students are able to develop full mediumistic abilities: they can see and sense spirit guides and relay messages from relatives, helpers and ascended masters in the spirit world. For some, this ability will stay on; for others, it will be a one-off. Just be open and see what comes your way.

The Connection Symbol

Meaning
The Connection Symbol (sometimes also called the Distant Symbol) helps us to realize the *State of Oneness.* We are tapping into quantum physics – the level where everything is interconnected. Every being is part of the same experience, and what happens to one has an effect on everyone. So, the Connection Symbol doesn't bridge space and time, it makes us aware that both are an *illusion.*

Oneness also means love. The origin and the goal of love are the same: to go beyond separation, to become *one.*

Visual representation
To illustrate the idea of original oneness and the illusion of separation, Mikao Usui combined five *kanji.* But he *literally* combined them: the ending of one *kanji* forms part of the next. So as soon as we separate the individual *kanji,* the meaning of the symbol is lost.

The Connection Symbol

Mantra

HON SHA ZE SHO NEN (pronounced 'Hon Shah Tsay Show Nen')

The mantra can be translated as: 'My original nature is a correct thought'[1] or, more simply, 'I see truth.'

Kotodama

(H)O-A-ZE-(H)O-NE (pronounced 'Ho ahh zay ho nay')

Use

To connect – with a person (partner, friend, colleague, client or even someone you don't particularly like), a situation (to send Reiki) or even an object. To connect with the past and the future. And in any situation where we feel lonely – or disconnected from ourselves. And of course it enables us to send a full Reiki treatment to anyone anywhere in the world. (*A step-by-step guide is on page 172.*)

It is also a great tool to use in meditation to connect to deeper levels of ourselves.

Exploring the symbols

The best way to explore the symbols is to *use* them. Apply them, play with them, see what works best for you. They can open a whole new world.

Exercise: Using the symbols with *Joshin Kokyu-Ho*

You can use any symbol (one at a time) together with the deep abdominal breathing technique (*Joshin Kokyu-Ho, page 129*) to become one with its energetic vibration.

❖ After connecting to Reiki, simply draw the symbol a few times and repeat the mantra (or chant the *kotodama*) and intend to breathe in Earth energy, heaven energy or the awareness of oneness.

❖ On the in-breath, fill your lungs with energy.

❖ On the out-breath, let it expand throughout your physical body and your aura.

Exercise: Introducing the symbols into Reiki treatments

The symbols can be used in various ways in a Reiki treatment. Use the Connection Symbol to connect deeply with the client before you begin the treatment (or halfway through if your mind has drifted off), the Power Symbol whenever you feel physical healing is needed and the Harmony Symbol when you feel the person needs guidance, or mental or emotional problems are involved.

Simply draw the symbol over the area in need or silently chant the *kotodama*.

Advanced techniques

Deepening intuition

There are two extraordinary Reiki methods of developing (or deepening) our intuition. In the first, we listen to our hands; in the second, we listen to spirit. We could say the first works on the principle of Earth energy, the second on heaven energy.

Exercise: *Byosen Reikan-Ho* (Body-scanning)

Byosen is a key word in Japanese Reiki, but apparently cannot be found in any dictionary. It is Reiki-specific and means 'that which is there before an illness'. It points to an area of the physical or energy body where toxins have accumulated. To find such an area, do the following:

❖   Sit or stand next to the recipient.

❖ Connect to Reiki, then take a moment to centre yourself and sense the connection to Reiki. (Some people then draw the Power Symbol on each palm. But this is optional.)

❖ When you're ready, state to yourself that you are about to start a *Byosen* body scan.

❖ Place either both or just one of your hands about 10cm (4 in) away from the recipient's body and move it down slowly, starting at the head. You may make side-to-side movements to cover the entire body.

Byosen *scanning*

❖ Whenever you experience a *Hbiki* (a sensation in your hand), just leave your hands there and let the Reiki flow until the sensation gets less and you feel that enough Reiki has been drawn. Then you can carry on with the body scan, pausing at every area in need.

❖ Alternatively, you can make a mental note whenever you discover an area in need of Reiki and come back to these places when you have completed the body scan.

❖ You may want to finish by placing your hands in the *Gassho* position to thank Reiki – and wait for feedback from the client!

Exercise: *Reiji-Ho* (Guided by spirit)

In this exercise you place your hands intuitively – guided by spirit.

❖   Sit or stand next to the recipient.

❖   Spend a few moments centring yourself.

❖   Connect to Reiki and wait until you feel the connection.

❖   Bring your hands together in *Gassho* in front of your heart chakra and ask Reiki to give you an idea where to place your hands.

❖   Then move your hands up to your third eye, your brow chakra, and be open to what comes into your mind. Many practitioners now get a word or image in their head (you may hear the word 'heart', for example, or see the image of a knee) to indicate where Reiki is needed. Take as much time as you need to feel where your hands are drawn, then place your hands on the indicated area.

❖   Alternatively, you may just lower your hands and let them move to whichever area of the body they are drawn.

❖   Remain in this position until you intuitively feel that enough Reiki has flowed and then intuitively move to the next position.

Guided by spirit

❖ You can finish the treatment by smoothing down the recipient's aura.

❖ Then place your hands in the *Gassho* position to thank Reiki and wait for the client's feedback to see whether what you found resonates with them.

Beyond time and space

Enkaku Chiryo-Ho (Remote healing)

For many students, the ability to send a distant treatment is the most fascinating aspect of Reiki. Not only does it heal, but the recipient doesn't even have to be present!

On my courses, I place half of the group in one room, where they lie on treatment couches, and the other half in the neighbouring room, from where they send a Reiki treatment to their respective partners next door. To make it easier, I suggest using a teddy bear as a prompt to know where to place the hands (ears, eyes, throat, etc.), but it's perfectly possible to simply visualize the recipient. Many students get sensations that are as strong as if the client were physically present. They feel Reiki being more strongly drawn into some place than others and they often sense any emotional imbalances. The recipients also tend to feel sensations that are similar to a hands-on treatment.

The funniest experience I ever had on a course was one guy mentioning that he'd felt a bit of pressure around his throat while receiving the treatment. The girl sending the treatment got terribly embarrassed. It turned out that when she'd reached the throat area, she'd briefly nodded off and ended up leaning on the teddy's throat!

It's amazing how we notice everything once we're on the same wavelength as someone. So, although you can't do any harm giving Reiki, when you give a distant treatment, please don't behave any differently than you would if the client were physically present!

Straight after the course, every student is able to send Reiki anywhere in the world. I got this email a few weeks ago:

> *'After we finished the course I was up late chatting to a friend on the phone and she said, 'I have to go – my daughter is coughing so much, it sounds as if she is going to vomit.' So I asked her if she wouldn't mind me doing some distance Reiki on her. She had been coughing non-stop for over two hours. So I did the distance Reiki and felt like a pain in my abdomen and a word popped up: 'Constipated.' I finished and sent a message saying, 'Please let me know how she is feeling in the morning.' And she did, she said her daughter had stopped coughing within the hour, had had a very restful sleep and one of the first things she had said [in the morning] was 'Mummy, I need a poo!' She's two and a half years old and she hadn't had one the previous day, so it turned out she was a bit constipated.'*

Please note that a full distant treatment should only be sent with the recipient's consent. Otherwise, just send Reiki in general to *improve the situation*. But if you have consent, this is how to do it:

Exercise: The traditional Western method for distant healing

❖ Connect to Reiki.

❖ Draw the Connection Symbol in front of you while repeating the accompanying mantra three times.

❖ Intend to connect to the person receiving the treatment. Say their name and location; for example, 'I intend to connect to Aunt Mary in Sydney for this treatment.'

❖ Start sending Reiki, using your hands. You can either use all 12 hand positions, or a selection, or follow your intuition. Practitioners often find that remote healing is particularly intense and therefore needs less time than a treatment in person. Many remote treatments last 30 minutes instead of 45 or 60.

❖ When the treatment is finished, clap your hands with the intention of ending the energetic connection or just say to yourself, 'I am now ending this connection.'

❖ Finish by giving thanks in *Gassho*.

Variations

❖ *A timed treatment:* When you say the name and location of the person, add that the treatment should be received at a certain time, for example 4 p.m. local time.

❖ *A 'remote':* You can place your hands on a 'remote' while giving a treatment. Teddy bears, pillows, etc., can be used.

❖ *A photograph:* You can place your hands over a photograph of the person.

❖ *A piece of paper:* Write down the name and location or name and date of birth of the person on a piece of paper and hold your hands above it.

❖ *Visualization:* Visualize the recipient and feel your connection to them.

A phenomenon

One day you may get into the embarrassing situation of agreeing to send someone distance Reiki at a certain time – and then forgetting all about it. It gets really embarrassing, however, when you then receive a phone call thanking you for the treatment! It once happened to me, and all I managed to say was: 'Glad you liked it.' As soon as the person hung up, I sat down and sent the treatment, only I timed it *backwards*. The universe *knows* that a treatment is going to happen. After all, time is an illusion.

Changing your mind

Exercise: *Sei HeKi Chiryo-Ho* (Changing bad habits)

This Japanese technique can be used to change behaviour, bad habits or addictions.

It can be used on yourself or for treating others.

Treating others

❖ Help the client to create the affirmation they want to use. It should be positive and set in the present, for example, 'I accept my new colleague' or 'I exercise regularly.'

- ❖ Ask them to sit or lie down.

- ❖ Place your hands in *Gassho* and intend to connect to Reiki.

- ❖ Draw the Harmony Symbol in the air, repeat the mantra Sei HeKi three times and intend that Reiki will help the client to achieve their goal. (*Note: The exercise can also be done without the use of the symbol – traditionally, it is left out.*)

- ❖ Standing either behind or next to the client, place one hand on their forehead and the other on the lower back of their head.

- ❖ Ask the client to repeat the affirmation silently for about five minutes.

- ❖ Remove your hand from their forehead. Keep your other hand in place for a few minutes.

- ❖ Finish by giving thanks in *Gassho*.

Treating yourself

- ❖ Create an appropriate affirmation for yourself, then use the same sequence of hand positions.

Getting to the root of a problem

Byogen Chiryo-Ho (Getting to the root of a problem)

This technique is absolutely incredible! I teach it on Master courses and in some advanced workshops. Amazingly, when I first came across it in a seminar I was only taught half of the hand positions and it still worked! Yet another confirmation that the key to Reiki is intention, not technique...

Byo means 'illness' or 'problem', *gen* means 'cause' or 'root'. Always the doubter, when I first tried this technique in a workshop (in my very early Reiki days), I didn't think it could possibly work. Not expecting anything, I still followed the instructions and set my intention to get an idea of the cause of any problem the other person might be suffering from. After a while, I saw an image of a girl on a swing. She was playing – but on her own. I got the impression she felt lonely. And I saw a train moving rather fast – obviously something completely unrelated.

When I mentioned these images to the woman afterwards, she broke down in tears. She had been suppressing some childhood experiences for most of her life and they had come up for the first time in this treatment. She realized that she needed to deal with them so she could move on with her life. Maybe this was where the image of the train came in...

I've used this technique on many courses now and the results have never been anything less than stunning. Some people become absolutely psychic!

Exercise: *Byogen Chiryo-Ho* (Getting to the root of a problem)

❖ Ask the client to think about a problem they have. It can be physical, emotional or to do with their life circumstances. I find it easier to be completely open if they don't tell me what it is, but this is up to you. Sometimes you'll know anyway and will use this technique to find the root cause of a specific problem.

❖ Ask the client to lie down on a treatment couch, relax and intend to get an idea of the cause of their problem.

❖ Now prepare yourself for the treatment. Connect to Reiki and ask that your client and/or you may receive some guidance on what has caused the problem.

❖ Place one hand underneath the person's neck and the other in front of their throat (but don't touch them, as this may be uncomfortable for them). Hold the position for about five minutes.

❖ Then place both hands on their crown (either next to each other or one hand on top of the other). Hold the position for about five minutes.

❖ Finally, place one hand on their stomach and the other on their intestines (just below the stomach). Again, hold this position for about five minutes.

❖ Finish by brushing down the aura, then thank Reiki and let the client know that the treatment is now complete.

❖ Allow them slowly to come back to the here and now – and exchange feedback!

I learned this version at a seminar. It worked brilliantly and I've used it ever since. My surprise, therefore, was all the more profound when I found out that this wasn't the original version! Traditionally, there are more hand positions:

❖ The forehead.

❖ The temples.

❖ The back of the head.

❖ The neck.

❖ The throat.

❖   The top of the head.

❖   The stomach and intestines.

The choice is yours – both techniques work.

Exercise: *Genetsu-Ho* (Reducing fever)

It gets even more interesting, because the very same technique can also be used for reducing fever. The only difference is the *name* – confirming once again, and even more strikingly, that Reiki is about intention...

SUMMARY

❖   The Reiki symbols are tools to help us concentrate on the three levels of universal energy.

❖   A Reiki treatment can be sent over any distance, as well as to the past or future.

❖   When we give a treatment, Reiki will guide us to areas in need.

Chapter 10
Shinpiden/Reiki Mastery: Pure light

The title 'Reiki Master' is really a contradiction in terms. Mastering *universal energy*? *Me*? Well, it says so on my business card. But I am not a master of Reiki. When I think of someone that term would apply to, the only person who comes to mind is Jesus. He could heal any condition, even resurrect people from the dead, and his self-awareness was entirely based on the understanding that he was a child of God. He identified with truth rather than illusion. The universe was at his disposal. I am sure there are other figures of world history this applies to as well. But this state is not (normally) reached on a Reiki Master training course. And Mikao Usui would never have taken the title. Our knowledge about his life and teaching suggests that he knew he was still on a learning path.

The title 'Reiki Master' was actually only invented for a Western audience. When Dr Hayashi put together a graduation certificate for Hawayo Takata in 1938 (*see page 18*), he did it in English – and he was searching for a title that would be associated with completing the highest level of training in a discipline. That's why he chose 'Master'.

And this is indeed what this level is all about – in *technical* terms: providing all the tools and theory available in the system of Reiki so that the person can teach others.

The Master level

There are several formats for Reiki Master training, from online and one-day courses (neither of which I feel are terribly profound) to three-day and week-long options. And the classic of Western Reiki training, a year-long apprenticeship (traditionally charged at US$10,000 and therefore increasingly less popular). Personally, I like the format of a residential course. Being plucked out my usual environment and fully concentrating on learning Reiki certainly worked best for me.

It may well happen, though, that we're not really ready for a course, or what we learn isn't as profound as we'd hoped. If this is the case, it's fine to take another Master course a while later. I took three, and every time I learned something new.

The Master Symbol

Meaning
The Master Symbol represents *enlightenment* – the realization of our true self.

Visual representation
This symbol, made of a number of *kanji*, is found in several esoteric Buddhist traditions in Japan and can be seen in

many temples (one of them being the current Buddhist temple at the foot of Mount Kurama). It's not certain whether Mikao Usui used it, but it represents the essence of Reiki perfectly.

The Master Symbol

Mantra

DAI KO MYO (pronounced 'Dye Koh Mee Oh')

The mantra is usually translated as: 'The Great Bright Light.'

Kotodama

A-I-KO-YO (pronounced 'Ahh eee koh eee-ohh')

Use

To sense our connection to the source of the universe, to feel the light within. It can be used in meditation, together with *Joshin Kokyu-Ho*, and forms part of most attunement methods.

The Great Bright Light

Learning the tools and technicalities and being able to attune to Reiki is only one aspect of the Master training. The other – and main one – is to use these tools on *ourselves*. Becoming a Reiki Master means embarking on a journey of self-mastery. Or, rather, self-discovery – discovering our *true self*.

Becoming a Reiki Master is a lifelong task. A wonderful one! An absolutely incredible one! But a task nonetheless. The Japanese name for this level best describes what it is all about: *Shinpiden* – 'the mystery teachings'. It's about the mystery of Reiki. The mystery of the universe. The mystery of life. Where do we come from? Why are we here? What does Reiki connect us to? What is the universe all about? Is there something *beyond* it?

There are no simple answers – otherwise we wouldn't need to go through this incarnation! – but Reiki gives us a hint. There *is* something beyond. Beyond the veils of darkness and difficulty, there is … *light*. Any problem, any fear, any separation we may encounter in life is only a temporary experience.

And, as always in Reiki, this is not just theory – or wishful thinking. The deeper we go in our use of Reiki, the more we can feel our light within. Even others can sense it! Often in attunements, students notice light approaching when the Reiki teacher comes closer to them.

Of course, the Master training enables us to teach and attune others, which is a wonderfully rewarding thing to do. But most Reiki Masters never will, and that is okay too. Becoming a Reiki Master is mainly about ourselves – about our dedication and our journey. If we change ourselves, we can change the world.

This core realization isn't restricted to Reiki Mastery – it can be felt at every level. When we can sense the light within, we can share it. And brighten up the world.

SUMMARY

❖ The Master level is about the existential questions in life. The goal is to deepen our path to finding our true self.

❖ A Reiki Master can teach and attune.

❖ The Master Symbol stands for the essence of Reiki: the Great Bright Light.

Part III
NOTES FOR/FROM THE PRACTICE

'There may be one out of ten who believes in my method before a treatment. Most of them learn the benefit after the first treatment, then they believe in the method.'
MIKAO USUI

Reiki as a professional practice

Once we give professional Reiki treatments (in other words, once we *charge* for a treatment), we are running a business. And with it come responsibilities: insurance, taxation, legal requirements. You will need to know the basics of practice management, treatment reports, client consent and technical requirements. Please familiarize yourself with these before you start your practice. It tends to be far less complicated than it sounds – most of it is simply common sense.

And don't worry too much (the Reiki principle comes in handy here) – it will all fall into place. If you are meant to be a Reiki practitioner (and if you are considering this, I am sure you are), the universe will provide what's needed. The more we trust in it, the more open we are to receive guidance.

And there's no need to rush into giving up your day job. You can always offer Reiki treatments in the evenings or at weekends, or maybe two days a week and go part-time in your other job. Take it slowly if you want to.

Reiki and money

Many Reiki practitioners only give treatments to family and friends (and to themselves). Others venture out into becoming professional practitioners. In other words, they charge for their treatments. And that's perfectly okay! If they didn't, they'd have to earn their money elsewhere – and most likely not have enough time to give many Reiki treatments.

Interestingly, though, Reiki seems to be the therapy where people have the most reservations about treatment fees. And I'm not talking about the clients, but the practitioners! It's very rare that anyone learns Reiki for financial gain. And even if they start out with that aim, Reiki tends to bring so much additional value that the idea is quickly dropped. Everyone practising Reiki gets so much out of it for themselves that they end up feeling rather embarrassed charging others for treatment.

In fact, it seems right to say that we cannot actually charge for Reiki. After all, it flows for free. So I don't agree with the idea that we *have to* charge for a treatment as a means of energy exchange. It is, however, absolutely appropriate *if* we do. And we can certainly charge for our time.

Alternative treatments tend not to be cheap. In fact, many are repellently expensive and exclude normal earners from accessing them. Reiki tends to be at the very bottom end of charges, almost as if it were a poor relation. An hour of hypnosis, for example, often costs five times that of Reiki. The question is whether this is fair either.

It means that many practitioners end up offering other therapies as well as Reiki. But, looking at the results that Reiki achieves, it certainly doesn't have to hide behind other therapies. As long as it is within reason (which differs with location and circumstances), a practitioner should charge what they feel is necessary. Starving Reiki practitioners are of no benefit to anyone!

Some practitioners now charge different people different fees; for example, a standard price for a normal treatment and donation only for clients with serious illnesses or who could not afford the treatment otherwise. I find this really conveys the spirit of Reiki.

Mikao Usui would not of course have charged the earthquake victims he spent months treating, but he had to make a living and support his family, and may well have charged normal clients, and certainly for teaching.

My personal attitude to charging for Reiki has changed a lot over the years. I used to be so embarrassed to charge for treatments that for years I rarely asked for any money at all. Then one day I asked the mother of a girl I'd treated why she'd stopped asking me back. It turned out she felt awkward because I'd refused payment and she didn't want to 'take advantage'. My good intentions had resulted in the opposite of what I'd been hoping for! Today I encourage my students to charge adequately. The world needs Reiki! And if we are busy making money elsewhere, we cannot deliver it.

Incidentally, this also applies to Reiki teaching. I'm not aware of any other therapy that is as cheap to learn. The cost bears no relation to the profundity of the system. So, if you're looking to learn Reiki, please consider that the Reiki teacher also has to make a living.

Reiki for kids

Children love Reiki! All you need to do is to gently customize the treatment for them. When I gave a series of treatments to an eight-year-old cancer patient, I tried to create an experience that was as pleasant and normal as possible. She'd obviously suffered enough through hours of regular chemotherapy and I didn't want her to equate Reiki with 'boring' or 'taking my playtime away'.

I started with a little taster. Placing my hands on her shoulders, I asked what she felt.

'Very warm,' she said.

'This is Reiki,' I explained. 'It will help you with your problems.'

Explanation out of the way, she concentrated on a colouring book while receiving Reiki. But a few treatments on, this became boring and she was allowed to use her iPad. Thirty minutes added to her daily allowance of playing with it!

A few weeks later, I knew everything there was to know about cupcake decorating (which was what she was looking at on the iPad). And the little girl's condition had greatly improved.

One of my students has made Reiki part of the bedtime routine for her three children. In addition to a bedtime story and a goodnight kiss, they now get a few minutes of Reiki too – the younger ones five minutes, the older one ten minutes. Their mother just places her hands on their head or chest and they feel the loving warmth of Reiki and fall into the most peaceful sleep.

It's fabulous to grow up with Reiki! Whenever there's a problem, you can go to Mum or Dad, who will use their magic hands to make it better. Soon kids from the whole neighbourhood will queue for Supermum with healing hands!

One of my students' sons was so excited by his mother's Reiki that he told his entire class about it – including the teacher. Next time his mother picked him up from school, the teacher wanted to know more. In the end, she invited the mother to come in one morning and explain Reiki to the class! Of course, if this happens to you, there's no need to start with quantum physics and interconnectedness – just say that Reiki is energy that comes from the universe. Just as the rays of the sun bring light and warmth, so Reiki brings healing and happiness. It's as simple as that.

Kids of all ages can receive Reiki. They can even receive it before they are born! I've had quite a few fathers-to-be on my courses who wanted to be able to give Reiki to the child in the womb (and, of course, to the mother too). I've also trained expectant mothers – and it's a wonderful thing for them to be able to just place their hands on their belly and share Reiki with their child. It's absolutely safe to give Reiki treatments to women at any stage of a pregnancy. Though I tend to joke that, as a practitioner, you should then charge twice.

Reiki can also be used during childbirth. You can either send it remotely or be present in the delivery room. Or the mother can connect to Reiki herself before giving birth.

The Reiki can continue once the baby is born. There's no need for 12 hand positions with small infants – it's perfectly fine just to hold or cuddle a baby while giving Reiki. Or to place your hands above their cradle or bed.

When the baby is older, you can use one or two hand positions – whatever you feel guided to use. And later on you can give Reiki for every cut, bruise, scratch or emotional dent from the playground.

And then there will come a day when your child doesn't want to be touched any more – at least not by their parents! After all, they're a teenager now and need to be cool. Don't worry about this – and, more importantly, don't take it personally. And don't force Reiki onto your teenagers. When they need it, they will come to you.

One of my Master students reported that Reiki had completely changed her relationship with her 13-year-old foster son. To begin with, she'd sent him Reiki only remotely or in certain situations, but now he was coming and asking for it. And the atmosphere of the whole house had improved – even the dog had become friendlier!

Finally, if you are one of those people who is always worrying about the wellbeing of your kids (which, personally, I find a beautiful trait), Reiki will give you an incredible tool for helping them. Send Reiki after them when they go to school, send it to their exams, send it to their first experiences of falling in love...

Reiki and old age

It always fascinates me how Reiki is popular with absolutely every age group. At the Reiki Academy London, we run a project offering Reiki for free through charity AGE UK. For many of the elderly clients, the treatments offer a rare chance of finding relief from their worries and aches and pains. Often, these moments bring back happy memories and allow for peace and relaxation. And, of course, the benefits of physical healing don't stop with age, and many clients feel remarkably better.

A friend of mine gave Reiki to her dad, who had been suffering from dementia for years. Now in his eighties, he rarely recognized her and many well-meaning people had suggested moving him to a care home. But my friend was determined to look after him – just as he had done for her when she was a child. Following the Reiki treatment, he suddenly looked directly at her and, in full control of his speech and mental capacity, said her name and how grateful he was for her help. A few moments later he went back into his own world, somewhere between Earth and heaven. But this statement had made all the difference to her.

Reiki and the terminally ill

One day we will all die. Not even Reiki will spare us this. Thank God! Dying is completely natural. It is part of life. Our time on Earth is limited by the natural decay of our body, and the closer we get to the limit, the more difficult it tends to become. And yet letting go of life is a difficult and painful experience – for the dying as well as for those left behind.

Reiki helps with this process in amazing ways. The terminally ill often feel some relief from their pains and find more peace and acceptance in their situation. The benefits of Reiki are so renowned that a huge number of hospices are now looking for Reiki volunteers.

And Reiki helps friends and family as well. They can make the most of their loved one's remaining time – and feel really close to them.

Of course saying goodbye is a sad thing. It takes time to come to terms with this – sometimes a very long time. But the tangible proof of our Reiki experiences can help us to accept that there is more to life than this world. Once we open up to sensing our connection to the spirit world, we can look at death in a different way. It becomes a moment of transition.

Of all the Reiki stories I've heard, the one that had the deepest impact on me came from a couple I trained in Reiki. He had been diagnosed with skin cancer and given only a few weeks to live, but in the end he lived for another year. And a complete transformation took place. Initially he was a scientifically minded person who considered that life ended with death, but his Reiki experiences totally changed his view. When he realized it was time for him to go, he didn't say goodbye to his wife, but simply, 'See you on the other side.'

Hearing that was the proudest moment of my teaching career in Reiki.

Reiki and serious illnesses

Not all cancer ends in early death. There are many successful conventional and alternative therapies for it, and Reiki is known to have a huge impact.

Reiki also helps with other serious illnesses. While working on this book, I heard two accounts of how Reiki helped with liver diseases. As I don't believe in coincidence, I thought I was meant to write about them here.

One was about an Aids patient who was receiving regular treatments from one of my Master students. Just before Christmas, she sent me an email:

> 'He has HIV, diabetes, peripheral neuropathy, hepatitis (which has caused his liver to harden), depression, high blood pressure, a bad back, enlarged liver, aneurism .... in fact it's easier to say what the poor guy hasn't got.
>
> Anyway, he cannot take medication for his diseased liver because it could clash with his HIV medication and high blood pressure medication. Yesterday he told me he'd been undergoing tests on his liver and had ... received the results from his doctor that it was healing really well and almost back to normal function!! This can only be my Reiki!!! I am so delighted, as was he, and it's the best Christmas present for him and for me.'

The other account I heard was about a Reiki student who was also suffering from liver disfunction. Before starting with Reiki, the levels of ALT and Gamma GT enzymes in her blood were dangerously high. After seven months of daily self-treatments, they were in the lower levels of normal and the non-alcoholic fatty liver disease was gone.

So, don't be disheartened by the severity of somebody's condition. Reiki might well work against all odds.

Reiki and traditional Western medicine

The fact that there are now a significant number of hospitals offering Reiki says it all: it is perfectly fine to combine Reiki and traditional Western medicine. Having Reiki available might even lead to patients becoming a bit more discriminating when it comes to choosing the right therapy for them – carefully weighing up the benefits and disadvantages of both traditional and alternative treatments. There's no need to dismiss allopathic medicine completely.

Reiki and other complementary therapies

How does Reiki compare with other complementary therapies? To be honest, I can't say. I know what Reiki can do, but I'm not intimately familiar with every other alternative therapy out there. All I can say is that from the Reiki point of view, it complements other therapies perfectly.

And there's certainly no competition involved. Why shouldn't different therapies have similar benefits? There's no need to suggest that Reiki is better than other therapies. But, of course, we are often asked to explain why people should go for Reiki rather than another therapy. I tend to explain simply that Reiki has been proven to be beneficial for various conditions – and the best thing people can do is just try it for themselves.

But there is one main difference between Reiki and other complementary therapies: the spiritual component. Few therapies go as far as changing our attitude to life, or our circumstances, or allowing us to find meaning in our existence.

Clearing spaces and objects with Reiki

It is often asked whether Reiki can be used for space clearing. Of course it can! We often find stagnant energies in places, sometimes from centuries ago, or a disturbance from a drama that happened minutes before we walked in. I regularly use Reiki to cleanse hotel rooms from such energies, but a new home or car may also benefit from it.

Although space clearing wasn't part of the original system, it's easy to come up with creative ideas. The simplest (which can be used straight after Reiki 1) is to sit or stand in the middle of a room, connect to Reiki, intend that it clears the room of any negativity – and then let it stream out of your hands until you feel all the negativity has dissipated. This can take anything between two and 10 minutes.

After Reiki 2, many students use another method. This is also simple. Just draw the Power Symbol in every corner of the room while intending to remove negative energy, then draw it up towards the ceiling and finally down over the floor. Afterwards, take a moment to sense whether all negativity has gone. If not, start again.

Should ever you feel that any negative energies remain, of course you can ask (and trust) Reiki to protect you. Or you can take this as a sign that you shouldn't be there and follow your intuition and leave.

197

You may also find that Reiki makes you more aware of energetic imbalances in physical spaces like your home or workplace. Just as in *feng shui*, you may feel drawn to move some furniture around. You might not want to sleep under a beam or have the sharp corner of a table facing you, for example. If it feels better, it will be better.

Frank Arjava Petter recalls that Japanese Reiki teacher Chiyoko Yamaguchi didn't use any of the above methods.[1] When she wanted to bring good energy into a space, she hung a scroll with the Reiki principles on a wall. Words carry energy...

Reiki can also be used to 'cleanse' objects. You may buy a toy or an article of clothing in a charity shop, purchase an antique or even inherit an item and then suddenly feel strange when you unwrap it at home. If so, just place your hands on or around it for a while and give it Reiki – or make some sweeping movements similar to *Kenyoku-Ho* along each side of it. Some people also 'cut the energy' by swiftly cutting through the air above the object three times with their dominant hand.

Reiki and religions

I once received a concerned phone call from a lady who had booked her mother on a Reiki course and was now having second thoughts. The mother was a devout Christian and was concerned that Reiki might contradict her beliefs. I must have been convincing enough in my reply, since she decided to turn up. And loved it! I've rarely seen such excitement in a student throughout the entire course. During the attunement she felt she was getting closer to Jesus. In the end she was convinced that Reiki was Christian at heart.

Another student was a Muslim. He was so amazed by the similarities between the Reiki philosophy and the religious teachings he followed that he intended to combine Reiki with his prayers in future.

Hindus often remark that Reiki allows them to deepen their devotional practices, while Buddhists say it enhances their meditation. And several of the Reiki Masters I have trained are Jewish.

Angels, spirit guides, religious founders and ideas of God, as well as light, peace, love and meaning, often come up in connection with Reiki experiences. Even die-hard agnostics used words like 'love', 'peace', 'depth' and 'quantum-level energy'. While avoiding religious terminology, these words really mean the same.

Reiki was specifically designed *not* to be directly associated with any one religion. Buddhist, Taoist and even Christian influences can be seen in it, but it has stayed open to all. Just as the term 'universal' implies we are all part of the same universe, so every religion is too. No matter how different their terminology may be, they all ask the same questions: why are we here? Where are we coming from? Is there a higher power in the world? Reiki asks those questions too – and points us towards an answer.

Reiki works with any religious belief, as long as it is peaceful and non-exclusive (and if it is not, the religion is not a true expression of what it was originally meant to be). Reiki works on the idea of interconnectedness. And this goes beyond any religious divide.

Reiki and relationships

As a child, I saw marriage as something meant to last a lifetime. I thought of the divorces of my friends' parents as oddities – after all, my parents stayed together. In my teens, though, I occasionally wondered whether their relationship was as perfect as it might be. In my twenties, I actively encouraged them to divorce. After 37 years, they finally did so. And they have been best friends ever since.

Not every loving relationship is meant to last. Interestingly, this view seems to be shared by Reiki. It can help heal a relationship – or give us the strength to end it.

One of my students had a relationship which had been volatile (to say the least), due to her boyfriend's regular emotional outbursts. The evening after Reiki 1, she offered him a treatment, and to her surprise he accepted. He even liked it. The treatments became regular, the outbursts fewer. In fact, they almost stopped. Two weeks later his mother called my student. 'What is Reiki?' she asked. She barely recognized her own son any more. He was calm and approachable. 'He is really, well, *nice* now!'

Another student, who had completed Reiki 2, attended a Reiki Share a few months after his course. Smiling all over, he couldn't wait to tell me the news: 'Soon after the Reiki 2 course, I left my job. Got a divorce. And I'm moving back to Italy.'

Slightly hesitantly, I asked if this was all good news.

'Absolutely!' he said.

And this morning, before writing this chapter, I received an email from another Reiki student (so much for coincidence):

'The reason I subscribed [to Reiki 1] in the first place was because I was facing divorce. I still refuse to believe it. Somewhere in my heart I still hope that by doing Reiki I can find a way to save my marriage. I just feel I cannot give up my feelings yet. However on the Reiki course I felt as though I was in therapy and it helped me more than any psychologist.'

Reiki friends

The first few times, your friends and colleagues may find it rather 'original' when you tell them about the purple light you saw during an attunement, or the insight a client received when you gave them Reiki. The more you talk about these experiences, the more people around you will find you slightly odd. And frankly, I would have done 10 years ago! So you may eventually stop mentioning them and become more and more introvert. Or you may be too shy to talk about them in the first place.

This is where your Reiki friends come in! These are people who can relate to what you're saying and share your experiences. Together, you can try to make sense of them and explore Reiki more deeply.

So, one of the most important features of a Reiki course is the participants' list! Please stay in touch with one another. Or search on social media, or find a Reiki Share in your area. It's good to have Reiki friends.

SUMMARY

- ❖ You can go professional or you can stay private – there'll be no difference in the efficacy of Reiki.

- ❖ The more examples we look at, the more we find that Reiki is good for *everything*. There are no cautions or contraindications.

- ❖ Don't worry – just trust Reiki. The more you use it, the more feedback you'll get and the more convinced you'll be.

Afterword

Trying to finish the last few lines of this book, I was interrupted by a news alert: the recently negotiated truce in a civil war in Europe had just been broken. Hope had turned to tragedy, with dead, injured, bereaved and homeless on both sides. When I finally switched back to what I was doing, my eyes fell on the words: 'Just for today, do not be angry.' Reiki has its ways of bringing me back.

What could I do? I sent Reiki. And wondered what would have happened if people on both sides of the conflict had learned it. Can you kill with healing hands? Can you harm someone when you are aware that we are all connected?

Once we feel the light within, it is impossible not to realize that the very same light shines in the other person. In *every* other person.

I'm convinced that Reiki can change the world.

Let's start.

Appendix
The development of Reiki

The development of Usui's system after his death is connected with three names: the Gakkai, Dr Chujiro Hayashi and Hawayo Takata. The first is that of a Japanese organization, the second a Tokyo doctor and the third an American citizen – who secured the survival of Reiki and started its world tour through Hawaii, North America and the rest of the world. Until, in the 1990s, it finally returned to Japan.

The Usui Reiki Ryoho Gakkai

After Usui's death, the group of naval officers he had trained took it upon themselves to continue the practice. They formed the Usui Reiki Ryoho Gakkai (translated as Usui Reiki Healing Association) and Reiki experienced a tremendous surge in popularity. Within a decade, hundreds of thousands of Japanese people were practising it. Some estimates are as high as 1 million. Branches of the association were established in every major city and the system was used for both physical healing and self-development.

This success story came to a sudden end, however, when the Second World War broke out. The Japanese government started to question whether people with healing energy in their palms, promoting the concept of oneness and sensing an inner connection to the universe, would support the idea of joining the war and shooting other human beings. The Gakkai fell under suspicion and its members had to go into hiding.

Then the war came, millions of Japanese were killed and afterwards the country concentrated on rebuilding and economic success. Spirituality was largely forgotten and even today the word 'Reiki' is unknown to the majority of Japanese. The system would have become extinct had it not been for another development: a schism. One member of the Gakkai, Dr Hayashi, broke away.

Dr Hayashi and Mrs Takata

Dr Chujiro Hayashi, who is said to have trained originally as a medical doctor, was one of the group of naval officers and the youngest of Usui's 20 Reiki Masters. A founder member of the Gakkai, he was the author of a manual detailing the organs in the human body, common illnesses and suggested hand positions for Reiki students. But in the 1930s he decided to leave the organization and open his own Reiki clinic. This was a highly successful venture – contemporaries noted that the client list read like a who's who of Tokyo's establishment, including actors, authors and business leaders. In the clinic Dr Hayashi had 10 treatment couches and his speciality was having two practitioners working simultaneously on each client. (I now use this practice in some of my workshops: two people work intuitively on the same recipient. It's fascinating to watch the practitioners being drawn to the same places! And, of course, very reassuring, too.)

In 1936 Dr Hayashi was asked to take on a new client, an American lady who came as a medical emergency. And it was this encounter that guaranteed the survival of the system of Reiki. The lady's name was Hawayo Takata. Born in 1900 in Hawaii (hence the unusual first name given by her Japanese parents), she had recently lost her husband, was working hard to bring up her two children and had come to Tokyo on family business. Falling seriously ill there, she had been diagnosed with a tumour in her stomach, as well as a number of additional problems, and told she needed urgent surgery.

Then something strange happened: she was lying on the operating table when suddenly she heard a voice saying: 'No surgery necessary. No surgery necessary.' And it just wouldn't go away. Pondering what to do, she decided to ask the surgeon if he knew of an alternative to surgery. To her great surprise, he did – his wife was a student of Dr Hayashi! Mrs Takata was driven to his clinic straight away.

Dr Hayashi told her that she would need to come in on a daily basis for several weeks. Just one week later, the pain had gone, a few weeks on, the tumour had disappeared, and in a few months, all her medical problems had been cured. It isn't hard to imagine her amazement! Especially as, sensing a slight vibration and intense heat during one of her first sessions, she'd lifted the blanket to see what kind of device the practitioners were using – only to find them laughing out loud. Of course, there was no device – only hands. What she had felt was energy – the energy of the universe. She had to learn this method too!

Apparently offering Dr Hayashi all her money (*all!*) helped to convince him of her sincerity and he accepted her as a student – the first-ever foreigner to learn Reiki.

She stayed for half a year, living in Dr Hayashi's household and working as a volunteer in his practice. In the morning, she would treat clients in the clinic; in the afternoon, conduct home visits. Dr Hayashi trained her in Reiki 1 and 2, and when her training was complete, she returned to Hawaii and began to work as a Reiki practitioner herself.

A year later, in 1937–1938, Dr Hayashi visited her there. He stayed several months, giving treatments and Reiki courses and training Mrs Takata to the next level. Before he left, he awarded her with a certificate stating that she had been trained as a *Master of the Usui System of Natural Healing* – the first time that the Western title 'Master' had been adopted (rather than the Japanese *Shinpiden*). To make the certificate official, it was verified and stamped by a solicitor.

Soon after his return to Tokyo, though, Dr Hayashi found himself under pressure from the authorities. His Reiki practice, and particularly his extended visit to US territory, had raised their suspicions. Eventually he felt the pressure was untenable and in 1940 ended his life.

Then the war came – and afterwards Mrs Takata seems to have been convinced that she was the only Reiki Master to survive. Taking this very seriously, she made a huge effort to promote Reiki, offering treatments and teaching levels

1 and 2. After Pearl Harbor, this wasn't an easy task, given that the system was not only Buddhist-inspired but also Japanese! Still, in the end, her healing successes were just too convincing and she established a prosperous practice and teaching business. She also began to travel to the US mainland and Canada.

When she reached her seventies, she realized that it was time to secure the continuation of Reiki and finally began to train the Master level. When she died in 1980, she had trained 22 Reiki Masters. Through them, Reiki spread all over the globe – well over 90 per cent of Reiki practitioners world-wide have one of these 22 Masters in their lineage!

What she taught, however, wasn't entirely authentic. It isn't clear whether she introduced the changes herself or Dr Hayashi had already changed the system. But both promoted Reiki as an alternative therapy and focused on physical healing. As Hawayo Takata was a practising Buddhist, she may not have felt the need to include any of the philosophy in her courses. For the American public, however, she stressed Reiki's connections with Christianity – going so far as to invent the story that Usui was a Christian missionary who had been asked by a pupil how Jesus could heal. Lacking a convincing answer, he had made it his mission to find out – and discovered Reiki. These and various other stories were later found to be historically incorrect and this led to many Reiki students sincerely questioning the entire system. In addition, Mrs Takata introduced a set sequence of hand positions (utilizing the concept of chakras) for giving a treatment, rather than relying on intuition, and also changed the wording of the Reiki principles.

It may be that this focus on physical healing initially secured Reiki's popularity in the West, but at some stage practitioners felt there was something missing. And a strange development was set in motion: Reiki started to get 'add-ons'.

Reiki today

Reiki today is the story of moving away and being pulled back. Indeed, many Reiki students have moved away. Not from Reiki, but from the techniques and explanations they were given. After all, how was it possible for a system for physical healing to lead to psychic experiences, spiritual development and life improvements? So they started to look for answers in other esoteric traditions. Eventually they adopted not only various (often useful) theoretical concepts, but also new techniques and even new symbols. Crystals, visualizations and hypnotherapy were also often introduced, and the origins of Reiki were assumed to lie in a whole variety of places, from Atlantis to ancient Egypt.

Many of these techniques and traditions are useful healing modalities and can also be walked as spiritual paths. But they are not Reiki. Adding them obscured Reiki – and in quite a few cases radically changed it.

Fortunately, just in time to stop this from developing any further, the system of Reiki went back to its origins: to Japan. A few Western Reiki Masters began to teach it there and eventually were introduced to the memorial stone. Finally some written historical information! They were also put in touch with a few Japanese who still practised Reiki (most notably a lady called Chiyoko Yamaguchi) and it turned out that the Reiki Gakkai had survived all that time, and a few other Reiki practitioners were still practising independently. The knowledge gained from these sources (albeit, in the case of the Gakkai, rather reluctantly shared) threw a very different light on Usui's system. Here, the focus was on spiritual self-development and the palm healing was almost entirely based on intuition.

For many, it felt like two sides of a coin. But, as I said right at the beginning, by turning this over, the true depth of the system can be revealed. This is the opportunity we have today: to understand the history and spiritual foundations of Reiki and use the many practical techniques in our lives every day.

Different Reiki branches

Looking for Reiki on the internet can be very confusing. The last time I counted, I found about 70 different names and varieties. The vast majority of them have little or nothing to do with the Usui system of Reiki. But there are also just slight variations. Here are the main categories of what is on offer:

Traditional Usui Reiki

These are the branches of traditional Reiki that kept Mikao Usui's original system of Reiki to a large degree intact. Differences here are rather a matter of emphasis than of changing the basics. Although each teacher will have their own style, the essence of the system is the same and any student taught in one of these systems will be able to have similar experiences and produce similar effects. Unless mixed with other esoteric disciplines, these traditions are the most authentic. The main branches are:

- *Usui Shiki Ryoho*: Usui Natural Healing System; Western lineage/through Hawayo Takata; the world's main Reiki tradition.

- *Usui Reiki Ryoho*: Usui Spiritual Energy System; Japanese lineage/through the Reiki Gakkai.

- *Usui Reiki, Usui Universal Energy System or adaptations of these names:* Often used as contemporary names for *Usui Shiki Ryoho* and taught by many independent Reiki Masters.

- *Jikiden Rei*ki: 'Direct Transmission Reiki', following the teachings of Usui's student Dr Hayashi.

- *Gendai Reiki:* Created by Hiroshi Doi, a member of the Reiki Gakkai, combining the original teachings with some recent additions but keeping the essence of Reiki intact.

- *Komyo Reiki Kai:* Created by Hyakuten Inamoto, a Buddhist monk, who combined traditional Usui Reiki with Buddhist teachings and grasped the spiritual essence of Reiki very well.

- *Radiance Technique™:* Taught in sevel levels, this tradition was created by Barbara Webber Ray, one of Hawayo Takata's Master students. (Most of her other Masters, however, adopted *Usui Shiki Ryoho*.)

Offshoots

These are Usui Reiki with significant additions from other esoteric traditions. Because of this, some professional

Reiki associations do not consider those practising them as eligible for membership.

❖ *Usui/Tibetan Reiki:* Now often (and rather confusingly) renamed Usui Reiki, it adds symbols from Tibetan healing traditions. Reiki 1 and 2 are normally taught on one-day courses.

❖ *Tera-Mai™ Reiki/Seichem Reiki™:* A combination of Usui Reiki and ancient Egyptian symbols.

Namesakes

These are healing systems that have adopted the name Reiki but have *no connection* to Usui's teachings and lineage. Often hands are used and energy felt, and these traditions are regarded as valuable healing modalities. Many claim to be channelled and are said to work by connecting to spirit entities. The most prominent are:

❖ Karuna Reiki™

❖ Holy Fire Reiki

❖ Angelic Reiki

❖ Kundalini Reiki

Fiction

Many other systems found on the internet combine the name Reiki with fancy additions, and it seems rather clear that they are not meant seriously – but then, you never know on the internet!

References

Chapter 1: The history of Reiki

1. Stiene, Frans and Bronwen, *The Reiki Sourcebook*, O Books, revised edition, 2008, p.385. Thank you to Hyakuten Inamoto for the excellent translation of the Usui memorial stone that is used here and throughout the book.
2. Quoted *Shoden Manual*, International House of Reiki, 2010, p.44
3. Quoted Stiene, op. cit., p. 387
4. Quoted *Shoden Manual*, op. cit.
5. Quoted Stiene, op. cit., p.386

Chapter 2: Energy: The universe and the body

1. Accessed 24 June 2015

Chapter 3: Healing: Our body and our life

1. Klatt, Oliver, 'Reiki am Unfallkrankenhaus Berlin', *Reiki Magazin* 4, 2012, p.14

Chapter 6: *Shoden*/Reiki 1: Adjusting to the light

1. https://tools.skillsforhealth.org.uk/competence/show/html/id/2809/ (accessed June 2015)
2. Beckett, Don, *Reiki: The True Story*, Frog Ltd, 2009, p.41
3. Miles, Pamela, *Reiki: A Comprehensive Guide*, Jeremy P. Tarcher, 2006, p.118

Chapter 8: Principles and poetry: bringing the light into everyday life

1. Translation by Hyakuten Inamoto from Stiene, Frans and Bronwen, *The Reiki Sourcebook*, O Books, revised edition, 2008, p.387
2. Quoted Stiene, op. cit., p.387
3. Watkins *Mind Body Spirit* magazine 28, November 2011, p.16
4. Bolte Taylor, Jill, *My Stroke of Insight*, Hodder Paperbacks, 2009, p.146

Chapter 9: *Okuden*/Reiki 2: Shining brighter

1. Stiene, Frans and Bronwen, *The Reiki Sourcebook*, O Books, revised edition, 2008, p.101

Part III: Notes for/from the practice

1. Petter, Frank Arjava, *This is Reiki*, Lotus Press, 2012, p.114

Further reading

Ten good books on Reiki

Beckett, Don, *Reiki: The True Story*, Frog Ltd, 2009

Doi, Hiroshi, *Iyashino Gendai Reiki Ho: A Modern Reiki Method for Healing*, 1998, International Centre for Reiki Training, 2013; revised edition, Vision Publications, 2014

Fulton, Elizabeth, and Prasad, Kathleen, *Animal Reiki*, Piatkus, 2010

McKenzie, Eleanor, *The Reiki Bible*, Godsfield Press, 2009

Miles, Pamela, *Reiki: A Comprehensive Guide*, Jeremy P. Tarcher, 2006

Petter, Frank Arjava, *This Is Reiki*, Lotus Press, 2012

Quest, Penelope, *Reiki for Life*, Piatkus, 2002, revised edition, 2012

Stiene, Bronwen and Frans, *The Japanese Art of Reiki*; O Books, 2005

—, *The Reiki Sourcebook*, O Books, 2003; revised edition, 2008

Stiene, Frans, *The Inner Heart of Reiki: Rediscovering Your True Self*, AYNI Books, forthcoming, 2015

My personal top 10 spiritual books

Bolte Taylor, Jill, *My Stroke of Insight*, Hodder & Stoughton, 2008

Emoto, Masaru, *The Hidden Messages in Water*, Sunmark Publishing, Inc., 2001; trans. David A. Thayne, Beyond Words Publishing, 2004

Hanh, Thich Nhat, *Living Buddha, Living Christ*, Riverhead Books, 1995

Lao-tzu, *Tao Te Ching* (The Book of Tao), various editions and translations available

Maharaj, Sri Nisargadatta, *I am That*, Chetana Private Ltd, 1973

Renard, Gary, *The Disappearance of the Universe*, Fearless Books, 2003

Tolle, Eckhart, *A New Earth*, Michael Joseph Ltd, 2005

—, *The Power of Now*, New World Library, 1999

Walsch, Neale Donald, *Conversations with God*, Vols. 1–3, Hodder & Stoughton, 1997–1999

Weiss, Brian, *Many Lives, Many Masters*, Piatkus, 1994

Acknowledgements

My family

If I was only allowed to thank one person, I wouldn't have to think twice; it would be Mum. Without her I would be nowhere near where I am today. Her name Petra comes from petros – the Greek word for 'rock' – and this is what she has been throughout my life. Needless to say, she has also been very actively involved in editing this book. After all, she gave me my first Reiki course as a Christmas present!

I would like to thank Cosima, my wonderful sister, for her support and inspiration - as well as the occasional challenge. We are much more similar than we may sometimes think.

And, of course, Dad and his wife Ingeborg. Thank you so much for your heartfelt concern!

My teachers

Reiki is learned by doing – but also through good teachers. I would like to express my gratitude to my two main Reiki teachers:

Penelope Quest who not only introduced me to the idea of truly holistic healing, but also helped me to understand Reiki as a spiritual path.

And Frans Stiene who enabled me to understand the depth of the original Japanese teachings – and the amazing concept of heaven and earth energy, oneness and the light that shines through it all. He made me realize that I need to look no further than Reiki.

Thank you also to Oliver Klatt for teaching me Reiki 1 (and sharing the wonderful advice to start every day with a Reiki self-treatment) and to Frank Arjava Petter for sharing his fantastic research into the history of Reiki – and for many helpful comments on this manuscript.

My publishers

Finally, I would like to say thank you to my commissioning editor Amy Kiberd and the fantastic team of Hay House UK, working on all aspects of editing, realizing and marketing this book. A first book is something truly special.

Adapting the Reiki principle slightly, this is how I feel:

(not) just for today, I am very grateful.

Index

ABOUT THE AUTHOR

Torsten Alexander Lange is founder and director of the renowned Reiki Academy London where he teaches students from all over the world.

Born in Hamburg, Germany, Torsten had a brief stint studying Lutheran theology, then went on to obtain a degree in Political Sciences and, in his 20s, became involved in local politics. The business he set up to pay for his time at university eventually took over, and he moved to London and became an internationally successful entrepreneur and jewellery designer. Ten years on, he was made bankrupt and lost everything.

After years of struggling, the discovery of Reiki brought long-needed change – literally overnight. Torsten slowly began to realize that without the difficult years before, he would not have found the spiritual path.

Today, he dedicates his time to researching Reiki. He focuses on trying to uncover and understand the spiritual depth of the original system of Reiki, and how to apply these techniques and principles to modern everyday life. Torsten uses Reiki daily for himself, and feels privileged to be able to share the first-hand experiences of hundreds of students.

He blogs about Reiki and offers online videos and tutorials.

www.reikiacademylondon.com
www.reikiblog.com

HAY HOUSE BASICS
Online courses

If you're interested in finding out more about the topics that
matter most for improving your life, why not take a
Hay House Basics online course?

Each course is intended to provide a powerful introduction to a
core topic in the area of self-development or mind, body, spirit.
Presented by a renowned expert, each course includes:

**An overview of the topic,
including its application and benefits**

•

Video demonstrations of practical exercises

•

Meditations and visualizations to guide you

•

**Specially created text guides, available to
download for future reference**

Available at a special low price, these courses are
the ultimate route to a full spiritual life!

Find out more at **www.hayhousebasics.com**